WINTER *Butterflies*

Kenzie Janzen

Hoyal Creek Publishing, LLC
Meno, Oklahoma

Dedication

For my firstborn, Kate, and my rock steady husband,
Cedric.
Love.

Author's Note

All of the characters and the events in the book are real, and the latter happened during the stated time periods. A few names, job titles, and locations have been changed to protect the identities of individuals. Some of the dialogue and the text messages are not verbatim; however, they are accurate accounts of what was said or written at the time they occurred.

Table of Contents

Acknowledgments

The author pens the words, but the characters create the story. I could not have done this without my key characters: God, family, dear friends, and others who worked behind the scenes.

Each word was divinely inspired and inked with God's love. I served only as the messenger.

I appreciate my family for tolerating me during the writing process. Without my husband's patience (and help), the story would never have developed so perfectly. And without ALL of the kids, there would be no story.

I am grateful to my mother, my sister, and my brother, who supported me during the dark days. They are what family is all about.

I must recognize my friend Diane as a major player in the evolution of my story. She befriended me when I was at my lowest of lows. She introduced me to Kourtney. After all of the drama, Diane still lets me raid her snack basket and use her bathroom, even when she is not home.

And finally, thank you to other family members and friends who supported me and gave input along the way.

Prologue

Alone in the silence, I sat in an old rocking chair. For its age of nearly fifteen years, it looked exquisite. The cream fabric had nary a crayon mark or juice stain—or a memory, for that matter. I restlessly rocked away the days, wondering whether anything would ever break the quietness.

In the summer of 2010, I had moved back to the house I'd lived in as a teenager. The monstrosity spanned nearly four thousand square feet. It had never really suffered from abuse. The paint, the cabinetry, the fixtures, and the floors looked as new as the day the builders had installed them. Everything smelled the same, from the gardenia potpourri in the kitchen to my father's cologne in what was once his closet.

Now, all of it belonged to me. My father had passed on, and my mother had moved on. She had left every material thing behind, but the house seemed as empty as my heart. Its six bedrooms, three bathrooms, two dining rooms, and a plethora of bonus space could supply a growing family plenty of room to make memories. Yet like me, it sat alone and waited to be loved by tiny hands.

I wanted a big family; it had become an obsession. I coveted the memories my parents had made with my siblings and me. They had a story to tell.

I grew up in a modest family of five. My parents, siblings, and I formed our unit. I claimed the title of middle child. Thirteen years separated my older sister and my younger brother, but it did not prevent any of us from bonding. In fact, the age differences gave us each a role model to look up to or a sibling to protect. It was something I wished for my one and only daughter to have.

The only real shortcoming about my family that resonated into my adulthood was the lack of spiritual depth. We attended church regularly, but I considered us "Sunday morning Christians." If it was not Sunday, we did not set one foot in church or talk about anything related to it— unless we happened to be sitting around the dinner table, listening to Dad's memorized prayer that he recited at every meal. Even during Sunday morning service, I did all I could not to pay attention. I listened to the Bible stories and knew the commandments but did not know how to apply them. I worried more about what snack we would have after the sermon.

I accepted Jesus as my personal savior at the age of ten during a summer church camp. The camp counselors told me that life was so much better with Jesus in it, and I could go to heaven and see my friends and family someday. That seemed exciting enough to an impressionable tween. I vaguely knew what it meant to accept Jesus, but I lacked an understanding of how to live through Christ.

Then tragedy struck our family in the late winter of 1992 and made the whole God thing seem pointless. My grandfather and grandmother were doctoring livestock and used their pickup headlamps for lighting. The truck lurched forward, killing both of them.

The accident left me traumatized and confused about my supposedly loving God. It broke my heart. How could a caring God let freak accidents like that happen? No one ever told me that horrible tragedies could occur to Christians. Being a Christian seemed futile at the time. God had not prevented my grandparents' accident. I wanted to desert him, but the fire and brimstone sermons that I had heard in church had been seared into my brain. To a twelve-year-old, those seemed scarier than sticking it out with God. I took a chance and chose him.

After my grandparents' untimely and horrific death, I cautiously cultivated my trust and faith in God through my junior high and high school years. He did not seem so bad, after all. On graduating with honors from high school and with numerous college scholarships, I could not wait to tackle the world. God even strategically placed my future husband on the back pew of the church I attended. I sat by him, shared a hymnal, and we married a year later. Apparently, I missed the message about honoring God and my spouse, however, because neither ruled in my marriage. I did everything to dishonor those marital guidelines. After four tumultuous years, I became pregnant with our first child, Kate.

Around the same time, in February 2004, my fifty-six-year-old father fell ill with a rare, complex cancer. I had never seen my father in a weakened physical state. The fragility of life was evident, and for the first time, my spiritual life really bloomed. I came to know Jesus personally. I had never prayed and attended church so much in my entire life. I wanted him to save my dad, but I also wanted him to change me. I wanted to be a godly spouse and mother. Fourteen years after I accepted Jesus into my heart, I started to understand how to walk with him.

We were blessed with Kate in the fall of 2004, and for two years my father got to experience the joy of being a grandfather to her. I became pregnant with our second child the year after my father passed away. Having suffered through the loss of a parent, I felt blessed about our expanding family. I looked forward to naming the child after my dad. I had God, a loving husband, a great job, a nice house, one healthy child, and another on the way. Everything seemed perfect. I praised the Lord, thinking I had done everything right, which had pleased him. Having experienced my fair share of heartbreaks, I figured the blessings were raining down because I deserved them. I loved God and served him; therefore, I expected happiness.

Instead, God surprised me with my darkest days. My life became the epitome of Murphy's law. Whatever could go wrong, did. Pain and suffering followed me like my own shadow. I wondered whether I would ever experience joy again. I grasped for something that God repeatedly kept just out of my reach. I tried to fill the empty chasms in my life with everything but Jesus Christ. I loved him, but I was troubled by his unwillingness to yield to my desire for an instant fix—which forced me to yield to his demand to *be still*. I did not want to wait for him.

I faced many seemingly insurmountable obstacles. Some I overcame, and I patted myself on the back for a job well done. God took the blame for the failures. I convinced myself that God had abandoned me. Why would a sovereign God of grace and mercy allow so much hurt? I had many questions for God but never got answers. I shouted. I raged. I cried. I cursed. I loved. I loathed. I needed to know why God let me suffer. What did he need from me?

My spiritual clarity was muddled. I experienced a number of harrowing traumas before figuring out what the sovereignty of God really meant. I struggled extensively with that particular caveat in my relationship with him. God took without my permission; I had no say, no control. I could not understand why I had to walk through the fire again and again. I longed to rock another baby. I yearned for a family with enough children to fill up the empty rooms in our home. I needed to hear laughter and the pitter-patter of little feet. The silence in the grandiose house killed me.

My story of parenthood remained partially written in the family history book, and God stayed hidden, refusing to compromise on my demands and only revealing his will one page turn at a time.

one

Winter Blues

I hated winter. The short days and long, chilly nights depressed me. The season reminded me of death. It didn't help that everything appeared dead. The trees had been stripped of their luscious green leaves and were left naked, exposing their spindly branches, which often creaked and rattled in the blustery Oklahoma winds. The gardens that once bustled with butterflies, birds, and bees were silent. The flowers that produced a rainbow of vivid colors had disappeared and been replaced by heaps of decaying brown compost and leaf litter.

Events in my life always seemed to take a similar turn during this season. Freak accidents, cancer diagnoses, and my own personal crises made for a bitter time. We made a lot of history in the winter. It was that history I wanted to forget but that shaped my character in some form or another. I conditioned myself to expect the worst.

Winter had stolen my hope and joy one too many times, *but* it did have one perk—Christmas—when I could always manage to pull myself out of the slump. The weeks before Christmas electrified me. Lights and decorations adorned the town, the radio blasted familiar Christmas tunes, and our house smelled of savory baked goods that never lasted until Christmas morning. Family members traveled long distances to visit, and churches put on festive programs. I loved the hustle and bustle of gift shopping for my loved ones. That time of year could negate the other dreadful days of winter.

In 2007, I anticipated another glorious Christmas with my growing family. It would be extra special that year. My husband and I were expecting our second child. Excitement filled our house, despite my due date being about five months away.

Early on, I had a textbook pregnancy. I felt great. I overcame a few bouts of morning sickness and fatigue and planned to cruise through the second trimester. I had no reason to think otherwise. I had a perfect baby girl growing inside my womb. I felt wonderfully blessed.

Alas, the bleakness of winter ensnared me once again two weeks before Christmas. I went from floating on clouds to living in hell. A proverbial bolt of lightning jarred me from my slumber one evening. I woke up to a moist sensation in my underwear. It seemed I had wet myself. I often woke up and made quick trips to the toilet, but the urge did not wake me soon enough that night. I hurried to the bathroom only to discover blood, not urine, soaking through my pants and dripping on the floor.

"We have a problem!" I screamed.

Cedric, my husband, rushed over to determine the cause of my panic. A look of horror came over his face.

He had no medical training, but he knew blood during pregnancy was not good.

"It will be okay," he said, staying calm for both of us. "Let's go to the hospital."

My heart pounded. I was confused, angry, and sad. *Had God taken back the joy he had given us?*

Cedric gathered our three-year-old in a blanket and quickly drove us to the hospital. Traffic was light at two o'clock in the morning. We arrived in seven minutes and sat in the waiting area for an hour with all of the other people who had less pressing issues than mine. Scratches and colds did not seem very important to me at that moment. I assumed that a dying baby in my womb would have slightly higher priority.

"These people are idiots," I said to Cedric, as the rage built inside me.

After registering a drunk who had fallen and bumped his head, the nurse called me next.

Nice, I thought. *Triage or not, injuries due to drunkenness should automatically disqualify individuals from medical treatment.*

I was mad at everything and everyone. I was so consumed by my own suffering; I'd lost any sense of compassion for other people.

"What seems to be the problem this evening?" the nurse asked in a chipper voice that grated on me.

Doesn't she know my baby has died? I wanted to poke her eyes out. Since she was oblivious to my condition, though, screaming obscenities at her would be fruitless. I bottled up my anger.

"I'm bleeding," I said. "I think I'm having a miscarriage."

Ushered into another room with an examination table, I waited for the doctor as my blood was drawn. I stared blankly at the white ceiling tiles. The smell of antiseptic permeated the air. No one seemed to hurry in the emergency room.

What kind of problem does a person need to have to receive prompt treatment? I wondered.

The doctor ambled into the room, almost an hour later. "What are we seeing you for today?"

Good grief! Didn't people communicate? I did not want to say it again. Tears welled up in my eyes. My husband recognized my troubled look and answered for me.

"We think she is having a miscarriage," he said.

"Okay. Let's take a look." The doctor performed a quick, noninvasive exam. "I don't want to make things worse by poking and prodding. You are bleeding but not heavily. I'll order an ultrasound to determine the baby's status."

What was the point? I'd already convinced myself that she had died. Regardless, I accommodated them by drinking a quart of water before the ultrasound so that they could see the baby better. I wanted to punch the technician. She pushed the transducer into my abdomen so hard that if the baby was not already dead, she surely would be after that. I swear, the technician made it painful on purpose, probably because I'd gotten her out of bed very early in the morning. She checked everything except the baby. I was quite annoyed. My little girl's body lay lifeless inside me, and the lady wanted to examine my kidneys and fallopian tubes.

"I'll check the baby now," she said.

Well, thank you so much.

As her tiny body came into view, the room went silent. With a few clicks of buttons, the technician zoomed in on a beating heart.

Cedric and I looked at each other in shock. *How could it be?* We had known in our hearts that our baby had perished. We received a blessed surprise when she appeared on the screen, and her little heart beat at a normal rate. I maintained cautious optimism.

The nurse escorted me back to the exam room, where I received discharge instructions. My official diagnosis was a threatened miscarriage. That meant a chance for more bleeding; some of which could compromise my own health.

Terror overcame me. One episode had frightened me enough. I didn't think I could handle any more health problems. In my first pregnancy, I had not experienced any complications. I had been healthy my entire life. I had never once had stitches, broken bones, or surgery. Yet ironically, I suffered from hypochondria, and I lived in fear of getting a disease. I didn't need something else to worry about.

"Come back if you have any more bleeding," said the nurse.

Lucky me, I thought.

We drove home, weary and unsure of what battles, if any, lay ahead. I crashed on the couch for the remainder of the morning. Mainly, I cried. I could not sleep. I prayed to God, *Heal my body and let this pass from me. I beg of you to take the baby now if she is not going to live. I don't want to deal with more bleeding.*

I called my doctor once his office opened to inform him of what had happened.

"Come on in so we can check things out," he said.

Cedric had to work, so I went to see the doctor alone. The possibility of more bleeding made it difficult for me to concentrate, but my mental distraction blurred the monotony of the lonely, hour-long drive.

The appointment was merely a formality. My doctor wanted it on record that I had a problem. Another ultrasound and exam revealed the same diagnosis as the one performed in the wee morning hours: I had a living baby and an unknown cause of bleeding. The bleeding had subsided, however.

I felt better about the situation and was fairly convinced that God had answered my prayer and healed me within hours. My doctor reassured me that it was probably a fluke and that many women bled at some point during pregnancy. In passing, he mentioned bed rest.

"There is no proof bed rest saves pregnancies. It's more of a mental thing. Women feel they are helping the pregnancy by resting."

I wanted to do anything that could remotely help and keep me from bleeding, so I put myself on bed rest. I called my workplace to let them know I needed to take medical leave until the situation stabilized. The first day on the couch did not bother me. I refused to stay in our bed because of my negative association with it and bleeding. Cedric did the housework and cared for our daughter. It was hardly a vacation for me, though, and proved more stressful than I'd anticipated. I went from being super active and extremely independent to an invalid who depended on someone else for everything. I got up only to use the bathroom.

After several days of inactivity, I had another bleeding episode. It was much heavier than the first. *So much for an answered prayer.* Fear, depression, and anger loomed in my mind. I sensed myself slipping into a pit. I couldn't do anything to prevent my body from rejecting the pregnancy. I shuddered at the thought of lying there bleeding, unable to perform normal activities and enjoy life. God had betrayed me and hadn't helped when I'd asked.

As I lay on my bed of thorns, I searched the Bible for verses that applied to me. I prayed for God to let me hear his voice audibly. I needed some kind of reassurance but was met with silence. I cried until my eyes swelled shut and my head pounded. Two days passed and another episode occurred. That became the pattern: two or three days in between bleeds and each one more substantial than the last. Doubts about God and his love for me crept into my soul.

Tension mounted within my family. Cedric grew tired of playing nanny and maid, and he needed to return to work soon. He would get to escape reality. I had no escape. Since God seemed absent, I wanted to take things into my own hands. Out of desperation, I decided I would get an abortion.

I blubbered to my husband, "I can't do this anymore. I'm scared I will bleed to death. How much can a person bleed? What if it keeps going and I can't make it to the hospital? I'm too young to die! I don't want to die!"

"What do you want to do?" he questioned, raising his voice out of frustration. "There are no options but to wait. You are not in danger right now. You're the most important thing to me. If something wasn't right, we would address it."

I didn't waste any time answering his question. "I want an abortion," I blurted, sobbing after speaking such a vile word.

I had always believed that abortion was murder, but now that I was the one having a pregnancy crisis, my emotions took over. My concern about my own mortality and living long enough to care for my family seemed more important than an unborn, unknown baby.

My conscience got the better of me, however. I knew that aborting the baby would only end the physical suffering. I would still have a lifetime of mental and emotional baggage to lug around. What-ifs bounced around in my head like ping pong balls. *What if the bleeding stops? What if the baby is born full term and completely healthy?* I would not know unless I let it play out until the end. The thought of killing my child caused me to wail even more. I had no control, and it was the root of my fear.

After that incident, God decided to crank up his sovereignty just a notch and bombard me with more frequent and heavier bleeding episodes. I thought that surely my noble choice not to get an abortion would be met with divine favor, but apparently not. At sixteen weeks of pregnancy, I spent most of Christmas Eve on the toilet, crying as the blood drained out of my body.

Christmas Day came and went. Everyone pretended to enjoy the occasion for my benefit. A family member bought a baby outfit and gave it to me.

"Are you stupid?" I wanted to scream. Their clumsy gesture made me nauseous. Perhaps they were encouraging me to stay optimistic, but I was not in the mood.

My mother bought me a sign with the word *Miracles* scrolled across it. I rolled my eyes. *Right,* I thought. *Biblical miracles are ancient history. The raising of the dead and healing of the lame don't happen in the twenty-first century.* God had passed over our house. The sign, however, made a home above the television. I scoffed at it all day long. *What a joke!*

My mother and my siblings took turns caring for my daughter and me when my husband left town for work. I lived with my sister part of the time, and every car ride to her home resulted in a bleed. I became a shell of my former personality and distanced myself further from my family as the pregnancy progressed. I had no vision for the future, except to wonder what they would do if I died, and it saddened me. *Would they miss me? Would Cedric remarry and forget about me? Would my passing be too traumatizing for my daughter?*

I never felt as helpless and worthless as the day Kate smashed her finger by getting it stuck in a door. I lay on the couch with tears streaming down my face as I listened to her scream in pain while my sister pried the door open to free my child's finger.

Every day I prayed for God to take the baby and stop the bleeding. I spent night after night hardly moving, because every time I did, things got worse. I started to wear diapers so that I didn't need to get up for anything. With time, the bleeding got heavier. Eventually, there were no pads or diapers absorbent enough to contain the blood. I had to wrap bath towels around my pelvis and lay on giant pads.

Four weeks had passed since the first episode. My muscles atrophied. Acne riddled my pale skin. I spent my spare time scarring my face by nervously picking at it. To the doctor's dismay, my blood tests always came back immaculate. Considering the pints of blood I'd lost, he fancied me a medical marvel. Occasionally, I spent a few nights in the hospital, due to bleeds that would not cease right away. My doctor witnessed one bleeding episode in his office during my appointment. It looked like a war zone. I stood on a doggy potty-training pad while the blood poured out of me.

"That is impressive," said the doctor.

"Thanks." *Idiot.*

Frustrated at God and needing to find answers, I continued searching my Bible for anything that gave me hope. There were so many verses, and none of them screamed my name: "Hope for the future . . . ," "Ask and you shall receive . . . ," "His grace is sufficient."

The future seemed desolate. I must have asked for the wrong thing, and I didn't fully comprehend God's grace and how it benefited me. I did not understand God or his purpose. I had followed him faithfully before my health problems started. I went to church and accepted Jesus as my savior. It did not seem as if I had received much of a reward for my servitude. I wanted him to recognize me during my trial. I wanted him to know I still sought after him. I wanted him to consider the choice I'd made to try to salvage the pregnancy. I felt nonexistent to God and the world. Everyone continued on with their lives, while mine wasted away on a couch.

two

A Baby to Love

I had spent five solid weeks swimming around in a black hole, unsure where I was heading and wondering whether I would ever get out. Mentally, I had died. I waited only for my physical death, which seemed imminent.

With the month of January nearly over, there was no end to the bleeding. The twenty-eighth, in particular, troubled me. I passed super-size clots as large as golf balls and had a lot of cramping, which was constant and had increased in intensity throughout the day. I apprehensively got up to find my sister when suddenly my body began to shake uncontrollably. I could hardly walk because I had no strength in my muscles. As I stumbled into her room, I got lightheaded. I heard a whooshing sound in my ears from my heart forcing as much blood as possible to my head. My legs buckled. I grabbed onto a dresser to stop my fall.

"I need to go to the hospital," I said, barely able to speak to her. "Something's wrong."

"Do I need to call 911?" she asked, rushing over to support my body.

"Let's just go," I said. *So, this is what it is like to be dying.*

She attempted to call Cedric, but he was flying home from a business trip, and his phone was off. We quickly arrived at the emergency room.

"What's the reason for your visit?" asked the receptionist.

I practically lay on the counter, struggling to stand upright from the intense pain. My sister stood nearby to stabilize me.

"I think I'm in labor."

"How many weeks?"

"About twenty," I whispered through the tears.

Immediately, I was whisked off to labor and delivery in a wheelchair. Over the intercom, I could hear the receptionist paging the doctor *stat.*

Placed in a dark, cold room, I curled up in a fetal position on the bed. I moaned in pain and rolled back and forth, trying to find a comfortable spot. The nurse took my temperature; I had a fever. That was not a good sign. The doctor entered my room a short time later and discussed my options.

"You appear to be in labor and possibly going into shock. With your history of bleeding, painful cramping, and now fever, delivering the baby is the safest thing we can do."

I nodded in compliance; I had nothing left.

"The baby will not survive this early," the doctor said.

The situation was bittersweet. The pain and bleeding and worry and hopelessness were almost over. However, it also meant the end of my baby's life. She would no longer exist.

Within minutes, I was prepped and pushing. There was no medicine to dull the pain. I literally used my own blood, sweat, and tears. After two pushes, I had instant relief.

"It's a baby girl. There is no heartbeat," said the doctor. "Do you want to hold her?"

That question would haunt me for the rest of my life. All that I mustered up was a cowardly head shake *no*. That was it. I didn't comfort her or express how much I loved her. I turned my back on her and walked away, tossing her out like garbage. It was my defense mechanism, though. I did not want to bond with a baby I could not keep. I did not want any more torture. My decision sickened me with guilt. *What kind of mother have I become?*

My husband arrived a few hours after the delivery. He didn't seem fazed by the ordeal and expressed minimal grief.

"I'm just glad it's over," he said.

I did not blame him for his lack of sadness or sympathy, because I agreed. I looked forward to forgetting about the previous five weeks and getting on with life.

⌒∾⌒

About a week postpartum, I started searching for answers. How could something so traumatic happen to a perfectly healthy specimen such as myself? Neither my doctor nor his colleagues had any diagnostic conclusions.

"It was just a fluke."

"Occasionally, these things happen."

"There was probably something wrong with the baby."

"The odds of it happening again are nil."

It was typical doctor speak, but I found in it a ray of hope. I did not plan on another pregnancy for a while. I figured that given enough time, my body would bounce back. Things would be fine with the next one.

I felt on the mend, but I got another surprise that crippled my healing process. I developed a terrible headache that would not go away. It hurt from sun up to sun down. Over-the-counter medicines did not help. I called a family doctor to schedule an appointment; it would be a two-week wait. That was a long time to have a headache.

During that waiting period, I saw sporadic flashes of light in my vision. *Great.* I knew it was something bad. I panicked, but expressing my concern to Cedric fell on deaf ears.

"You are such a hypochondriac," he said. "You are not dying."

"I'm not exaggerating!" I screamed. In typical hypochondriac fashion, I searched for all possible causes on the Internet. *Of course, it was a stroke. I knew it!* That sent me into a frenzy.

"Let's take a drive to chill out," he said.

I thought that getting out of the house might do me some good. We went to a retail store to pick up a few things. I continued to see flashes of light, and my anxiety level increased with each one. I was familiar with stroke victims. Thanks to an ailing grandmother, I knew the symptoms, and I had two of them. All that I needed to find out was my blood pressure, to convince myself one way or the other.

I sought out a machine located in the store. I knew my pressure had been good at the hospital, so this was certain to ease my fears. I stuck my arm in the cuff and waited for the squeeze and release. The numbers appeared on the screen, 150/100. I froze with fear.

Cedric tried to console me. "The machine is probably broken. You are fine. Maybe you're just stressed out, and the numbers are higher at this moment."

His attempt to calm me down did not work. Once again I felt out of control. I'd thought that God would restore my life after sending me through hell. Why was the God I depended on for comfort, protection, and healing doing the complete opposite of what I needed? I had lost a baby and also apparently lost my health. If I ever had serious doubt about God's love, it was then.

I decided to secretly make a trip later in the evening to the emergency room to get some reassurance through testing and get on with my life. I told my husband I wanted to take a drive alone to clear my head. Night fell, and off I went in an attempt to regain control.

As I registered at the hospital, the nurse looked over my symptoms: headache, high blood pressure, and visual disturbances. I was immediately taken back to an exam room and hooked up to heart and blood pressure monitors. The doctor ordered a battery of blood tests, a urinalysis, and a CT scan of my head. Finally, someone paid attention to me. *It's about time.*

"Good news," said the doctor. "Every test came back normal. You are not having a stroke or any type of cerebro-vascular event. Your heart is fine, and your blood pressure is stable. You are just fine, but I would like to watch you overnight."

"Thank you," I said to him.

I called Cedric to tell him what I had done. He was not happy and refused to come to the emergency room to see me.

"There is nothing wrong with you, and I'm not coming up there. You have got to get a grip on this. You need to go to counseling or something. You can't run to doctors to have them fix a nonexistent condition."

I had no support from home.

The doctor popped in. "I talked with another doctor. We don't think it is necessary for you to stay. You are being discharged. Come back if anything changes."

The doctors had rejected me too. They were my last hope. I didn't feel fine. I had demons screaming inside me, telling me I was in danger of dying. I just wanted some-one to care. I wanted to feel safe. I wanted to feel God's presence.

I went home with my tail tucked between my legs. The house felt empty, even though Cedric and Kate played on the floor. I walked past them without speaking a word. I went to the bedroom, closed the door, and wept. I just wanted to die. Having no hope for anything and feeling unloved by everyone, including God, was no different than death.

three

No Way but Down

I spent days in bed, staring at the walls, which closed in more with each passing hour. I tried to keep my blood pressure down. I felt no motivation to get up, except for an occasional appointment. I had numerous prescriptions for depression and anxiety; I probably could have started my own pharmacy. Yet I hated mind-altering drugs. I saw them as a sign of weakness, so I never took any. I kept the room extremely cold and free of noise. The lights remained off, unless I was eating. I ate all of my meals in bed. Cedric tried to get me to do things, but I refused. I rolled away from him and sank deeper into the darkness.

Three weeks after the baby died, Cedric went away to work for the first time. He would be gone three days. I begged him not to go. I did not feel capable of caring for myself or our daughter. I hadn't done anything with her in two months; I wasn't a good mother. A sane woman would have relished the opportunity to care for her child after being absent from her daughter's life. I dreaded being alone with her, but not because she was a burden. I worried that something would happen to me, and she would end up by herself somewhere. I didn't want her to see me having a health crisis and be scarred by what she witnessed. I thought I was protecting her, but in reality I was still concerned about myself.

I said goodbye to Cedric and shut the door, with tears rolling down my cheeks. I couldn't look at my daughter. I ran to the cabinet and popped an anxiety pill. I didn't know what to expect or how I should feel. I didn't know whether it was safe to take the pill while alone with a child. I waited for some profound effect to occur.

I needed to do something to calm my nerves until the medicine kicked in, so I vacuumed. Pushing around a vacuum was trivial, but it changed my perspective. I appreciated the normalcy it brought to me, though I cried the entire time. I had surrendered to the sadness of losing the baby, the fear of losing my health, and the loneliness of being without support for long enough. I made a choice to vacuum, instead of going back to bed to wallow in self-pity. I finally took a small step forward and regained a tiny bit of control.

Friends invited Kate and me to a basketball game that night. I wasn't really interested, but it allowed us get out of the house. When the game was over, I didn't want to go back home. It had been a very stressful place for too long; I was traumatized and scared. I had my daughter sleep with me to serve as my *monster blanket*. I felt safe, even though I had only a three-year-old by my side.

We spent very little time in the house during the days. I moved a small television into the garage for entertainment to escape the confines of the house. We also people-watched at the fitness center for two or three hours in the evenings. I usually didn't return home until ten o'clock. I did a poor job of putting my daughter first. I sacrificed her routine because of my selfishness. I grasped at any activity I could do to stay away from home. I really hated the house. It was like returning to a prison cell and being locked up, again and again.

I thought that if I removed every memory of the pregnancy from the house, the stress would go away. I threw away pillows and blankets I had slept with, cups I had drunk out of, and ultrasound pictures of the baby. I wanted it all erased. I wanted the pain to disappear. My hasty decisions only proved futile and brought about more sorrow.

❧❦

In mid-February I received a phone call from work. My boss wanted to know when I was returning. I honestly hadn't thought about it. I hadn't heard from anyone since I had called to let them know I would be taking medical leave almost two months earlier.

"I need to know when you're coming back." His voice was not sympathetic. "You need to get back into a routine and put this behind you."

Thanks a lot. Jackass!

I was so angry. He had no clue what I had been going through. I really didn't want to go back, but I feared I might lose my job, so I blurted out, "I guess I can come back Monday."

Monday was three days away. I certainly wasn't mentally ready, and I felt sick to my stomach having said that. As a teacher, I wondered how I could get through a day surrounded by half-crazed, hormonal teenagers. I had my own drama to deal with, and I didn't need anyone else's.

For the next couple of days, I swam in a pool of angst that threatened to drown me. Cedric finally returned on Sunday to take over. Less than a day away from rejoining the workforce, I paced around the house, from one room to the next. The faster I moved, the greater the chance I could escape my fears. I breathed as if I had ran a marathon. My nerves were shot.

I briefly paused in our spare bedroom, which we had planned to make the nursery. We had stripped the walls of pictures, in preparation for hanging baby decorations, which never happened. The room remained barren and empty, much like me. I noticed several framed pieces that had once adorned the walls now sitting on the dresser. One in particular caught my attention—a rather lengthy inscription that made the shape of a large footprint. I had purchased the print myself. The colors of the frame and the mat went well with the rest of the room's decor. The beach scene in the background was an added bonus. I hadn't bought it for the written inscription but for its aesthetics. In fact, I'd never really bothered to read it. The title was *Footprints in the Sand*. I carefully read each word.

One night a man had a dream. He dreamed he was walking along the beach with the LORD. Across the sky flashed scenes from his life. For each scene, he noticed two sets of footprints in the sand: one belonging to him, and the other to the LORD. When the last scene of his life flashed before him, he looked back at the footprints in the sand. He noticed that many times along the path of this life there was only one set of footprints. He also noticed that it happened at the very lowest and saddest times in his life. This really bothered him and he questioned the LORD about it. "LORD, you said that once I decided to follow you, you'd walk with me all the way. But I have noticed that during the most troublesome times in my life, there is only one set of footprints. I don't understand why when I needed you the most you would leave me." The LORD replied, "My son, my precious child, I love you and I would never leave you. During your times of trial and suffering, when you see only one set of footprints, it was then that I carried you." ("Footprints," author unknown)

As the words soaked into my weary soul, I felt the demons release their grip. My body melted into a pile of mush. It was the first time in a while that my vulnerability was eclipsed by a feeling of security, my weakness was overcome by strength, and my emptiness was filled with an overwhelming sense of love. *Was it God? Had he carried me just as a mother carries her young—just as I had carried my baby until God took her away from me?*

I fell to the floor and burst into tears. I was overcome with sadness because of the death of my child, yet relieved that God had not abandoned me. I was encouraged by his presence but still frustrated that he hadn't done something to save my baby and make it obvious that he had been with me. The array of emotions I felt made me very confused. I questioned whether I'd ever had an intimate relationship with God. Maybe that explained why I felt he was absent during my pregnancy. It required more than one poetic revelation to convince me. I didn't need proof God existed; I believed in him. I wanted proof that his nature was one of love, as I had learned in the past.

I demanded answers. Why did he need my baby? Why did I need to hurt? What was his purpose?

four

A New Friend

The day I returned to work came too soon. At 7:00 a.m., I was awakened by the obnoxious beeping of my alarm. My old anxiety tugged at me, telling me to stay safe in bed. However, the threat of an angry boss calling me crushed it. Getting myself ready reminded me of dressing a toddler. My mind resisted the change that was taking place. I wrestled with my clothes, hair, and makeup. I tried to look as professional as possible, yet I had grown accustomed to looking in the mirror and seeing the reflection of an unkempt, worthless weakling trapped in the bondage of depression and anxiety.

My stomach had gone topsy-turvy, so breakfast was out of the question. I collapsed on the couch as if I had just come home from a day's work, and it wasn't even eight o'clock. Overwhelmed to the point of tears, I felt as if it was my first day of kindergarten. I was the scared little girl who clung to the pant legs of her parents—except that Cedric had inherited the parental role.

"You are going to be fine. You can call me if you need something. You are stronger than you know."

He gave me a reassuring hug. I didn't want to let him go. He walked me to the car and practically forced me in. I rolled down the window, and he grasped my hand and gave it one final squeeze. I could barely see through my tears. It was time to go.

I bawled during the entire thirty-minute drive. I wanted to move forward with my life so badly, but I was afraid. The future held too many unknowns that worried me, considering the shocks of the past. When I arrived at the school, I sat in the parking lot for a few minutes to compose myself. My face had turned scarlet red, and black mascara streaks ran down each cheek. *So much for professional.* I half-heartedly asked God to get me through the day.

I checked in at the office and was greeted by a few coworkers, who awkwardly extended their condolences. I didn't fault them, however. "Sorry your baby died" just did not have a nice ring to it, no matter how sympathetically it was said.

Surprisingly, my boss invited me into his office. Contrary to his demeanor on the phone a few days earlier, he exhibited gentleness and expressed his concern.

"If you need a break or someplace to chill out, just come to my office. The door is open."

What? I barely saw eye to eye with this guy on anything. He was a pompous jerk, and I had completely avoided him in the past. I was flabbergasted at his hospitality.

"It's good that you are back. We'll get you into a routine. It will be good for you."

His kindness was too much. I didn't know what to say. *Just when you think you know a person!* I choked back the tears and said thank you.

I trudged on to my classroom with my senses in overdrive. I had walked the hall hundreds of times and usually tuned out lockers slamming, kids discussing stuff I didn't want to know about, and the smell of cafeteria food that permeated every possible niche. That day this sensory bombardment couldn't be ignored. I could even hear the distinct sound of a lady's heels, clopping rapidly behind me in the distance.

I entered my dark classroom and flipped on the light. It was dank and smelled musty. The fluorescent lights buzzed and flickered. In the hall the clopping heels were much louder and slowed as they neared my door. The secretary I had seen many times before, but hardly talked to at all, invaded my territory as if it belonged to her. Once she entered, I wouldn't be getting her out, *ever*. I didn't know it at the time, but she would play a pivotal role in my future.

Diane extended her arms to give me a hug. It was awkward because I barely knew her.

"I'm so very sorry," she said. "I don't know what you are going through, but I have been and will be praying for you. If you need anything like a break from class or someone to talk to, please come to me."

Her sincerity hit me and turned on the water works. *Seriously, what is the deal with all the compassion?* I relaxed just a bit with the thought that I had options to escape if I needed them.

"Thank you," I said.

The bell rang just as she left. The students jostled into the classroom. I had no idea what I was going to teach. I would have to wing it. I fancied myself well organized, so it was a new experience. The students sat in the seats I had assigned to them months ago. Their faces wore expressions of business as usual. They apparently hadn't skipped a beat in my absence. I sort of hoped that a few of them would approach my desk to give me their condolences or a homemade card. There was nothing of the sort. I shouldn't have been offended, considering that they were narcissistic teenagers consumed by their own world of zits, gossip, and body odor. Most of them hadn't known I was pregnant; therefore, I had not been on their minds. It was probably for the best. At least I didn't have to answer TMI (too much information) questions that students loved to ask.

I sensed an uncomfortable silence spreading through the classroom. I knew it was my job to break it. I opened the textbook to the marked page the substitute teacher had left for me and started lecturing. I was a writer and a speaker, so I always had prewritten notes on the whiteboard for the students to copy.

I hated to turn my back on the kids, for obvious reasons. An occasional paper airplane flew or love note passed if I wasn't watching with one eye. That day I turned away from the students, lacking concern about anything. I just wasn't into it. I kept feeling a chill or a tingling sensation on my right arm and cheek, and it rattled my nerves. I'd thought that the health ailment paranoia had passed, but

I became more focused on the tingling. Soon I felt short of breath.

I am going to stroke out right in front of the students. I abruptly stopped the lecture, sat down, and tried to catch my breath. I needed air. I frantically flipped to the end-of-chapter review and assigned it to the students. I had to distract them so that I could figure out what was going on with me.

The bell rang and the students dashed out. *Maybe they didn't notice my panic.* I nervously hurried down the hall packed with students. I was cold and couldn't breathe.

I reached the office and motioned for Diane to follow me. She immediately left her tasks behind, put her hand on my shoulder, and together we went into a private office.

I could barely speak to tell her what was wrong. I breathed hard and fast. Holding back tears, I squeaked, "I can't do this."

She used the phone to call back to the main office and have someone cover my classes for a few minutes.

"What happened?" she asked me.

"I swear I am having a stroke. My cheek and arm are tingly. I think I am dying."

"You are going to die," she said bluntly. "But not today and not anytime soon. You are having a panic attack. Take deep breaths in through your nose and out through your mouth."

I could only sob. I wanted to go, but I didn't know where. There seemed to be no safe place anywhere for me to hide.

Diane tried to redirect my attention by telling her own harrowing story. Though I kept crying, I listened.

"Five years ago I was diagnosed with breast cancer," Diane said. "The day I was diagnosed I was numb and felt like the air had been sucked out of me. There were no words that would make it go away. I was worried about my kids and grandkids and how they would cope if I were to die. I wanted the cancer out of my body so I could feel like my old self, but I never got my old life back. Trauma changes a person. It changes your soul. You see life in a new way, sometimes for the better and sometimes for the worse. *This* is the one thing you can control. You can be angry and bitter, or you can grab on to the precious time God has given you and leave behind a legacy your family can be proud of. I'm living proof that in every bad experience there can be good. God obviously let me beat cancer so that I could be here to help you and give you hope. God has a reason for your trials and a reason for you. This, too, shall pass. Someday you will be able to share your story with someone and give that person hope."

A lady whom I didn't know that well had shared an intimate part of her life with me, a mental case. What echoed in my head the most was that I had a choice to make. I could control my thoughts and actions. She hadn't been forced to care about me or take time to talk. We didn't have any history together whatsoever. She reminded me of being with my mother when I was scared as a child. I felt safe. I liked her. She hadn't judged me.

She was honest, forthcoming, and kind. I felt a connection to her.

She gave me a pat on the back, then I walked in one direction and she in the other. Our brief interaction was the beginning of a friendship that would have many twists and turns beyond my imagination.

five

The Redeeming Chicken

I lumbered through the school days, spending any free time I had in Diane's office. Having a new friend comforted me.

I faced a new challenge in my workplace, though. A coworker, who was also a friend, had announced her pregnancy. I had a very difficult time seeing her glowing face and expanding waistline. *She already has three kids, why does she get another?* It evoked so much bitterness and jealousy in me that every baby I saw and every pregnant woman in my presence received a sour reaction. My heart ached. Robbed of the joy of having my own baby, I viewed any pregnant woman as an enemy, and I wanted nothing to do with her. I avoided my coworker whenever possible. I was angry at God, because it seemed as if he was just rubbing it in my face. Life around me moved on, and I felt stuck in the past, waiting for God to endow me with some sort of triumphant reward to make up for my loss.

Spring was upon us, and the school year got very busy with sports, band contests, and state testing. I looked forward to seeing flowers in bloom, as well as the butterflies that fluttered around them without a care . . . content all of the time. I hadn't experienced contentment for a while. It was almost as if butterflies were specifically designed to bring peace to restless, aching hearts. Their grace and beauty made everything seem . . . okay. Spring signified a new beginning.

One of my classes incubated chicken eggs as a project. They were very close to hatching. I had to go to school every day of spring break to turn the eggs. I didn't mind, because it gave me a routine and kept me away from the house. The day the chicks hatched was very special. I had cared for them for several weeks. In a weird, psychotic sort of way, it was like a pregnancy do-over. It was therapeutic. One by one, the chicks hatched and entered a brand-new world. To ensure their survival, I maintained the perfect temperature, provided fresh water, and gave ample food.

I took a liking to one chick in particular. It had issues with standing and walking. The next few days I watched the chicks acclimate to their surroundings. They ate and moved well, except for the one. It was much weaker than the others. It tried to get up and walk to the food, but its legs splayed out, and it fell over, time and time again. A coworker and his wife came by to check on the chicks.

"That one is probably going to die," he said.

His wife chimed in. "Yep, it is a runt. It won't make it."

I furrowed my brow and glared at them. "Well, maybe if it were left up to you. But I am going to try to save it."

I was upset at their lack of compassion concerning a weaker creature. I couldn't understand why they didn't care about that poor baby. They just didn't get it. I was more determined than ever to save the chick.

With all sorts of scientific equipment at my disposal, there had to be something I could construct to keep the chick upright. I thought for a minute. There in front of me was a box of rubber hoses of various sizes, and to my right hung a first aid kit on the wall.

This chick is getting some leg braces! I thought.

I picked a hose with a diameter wide enough to wrap around one of the chick's legs, then I cut two chick-size pieces. I made vertical slits in the sides so that I could place them around its legs. I used two small bandages from the first aid kit to loosely fasten the hose pieces together. The device kept the legs positioned normally so that the chick could walk without stumbling. It was genius—at least, I thought so.

I took the chicks home so that I could monitor them more closely. They lived in a small box in our kitchen. It was redneck. Kate and I both loved it, but Cedric got tired of hearing the chicks fuss all night. Like a new mother learning her baby's cry, I learned the lame chick's peep. It would make all sorts of racket when it fell over, but it figured out how to erect itself by pushing up with its wing. The chick adapted to its new braces and motored around exactly like the rest of the brood.

Several weeks passed, and it was time to do a test run without the braces. I removed the bandages so that the chick's legs could move completely unhindered. With one successful step after another, the chick made me one proud momma. I'd done it. To most people, it was just another chicken to eat, but not to me. It gave me an opportunity to save a life. It mirrored what I'd wanted to do so badly with my own baby. I got to be a mom again. It made for a bittersweet memory but one of satisfaction.

꼶꼶

In late April, state testing was finally over. For the most part, we were on cruise control. With more time on my hands, I made the decision to attend counseling to try to get my life back. Anxiety continued to plague me; however, keeping myself occupied with my chicken herd helped tremendously.

The counselor diagnosed me with post-traumatic stress disorder (PTSD). I thought the condition affected only military veterans who had served in wars, but, apparently, anyone who experienced a trauma could succumb to PTSD. I had a label and got the help I needed. I met with the counselor many times, which eventually forced me to reveal the guilt I carried for not having held the baby. That in particular had eaten away at me. I exposed my fears of dying and leaving my family behind, my grief over losing a child, and my anger at God for putting me through physical, emotional, and mental pain. After months of counseling, I graduated to my new normal. I had not forgotten the past, but I could cope with it and feel positive about the future.

To commemorate the occasion and to remember our baby, the counselor suggested that we plant a tree. It just so happened that my daughter's daycare was teaching the children about conservation and had given each child a pine sapling to plant. Cedric and I drove out to the family farm and planted it in the middle of the garden. Merely four inches tall, it paled in comparison to the giant red cedars and oaks that towered overhead. It was the only one of its kind. Without cohorts, surviving the gusty Oklahoma winds or the deer that loved eating small trees would be a challenge. We swaddled it with burlap and a wire cage and quenched its thirst with cold well water. We said a prayer to God for peace and healing. We turned around and walked away, leaving behind the little tree, as well as a piece of our hearts. We chose to name the tree in honor of our baby. Reece grew over ten feet tall in five years. Our baby's memory lived on.

six

Growing in Faith

As the school year came to its official close in May 2008, I made an appointment with my doctor to take a closer look at my reproductive organs. He wanted to verify whether things were healthy and it was safe to pursue another pregnancy. I didn't want to be probed any more than I had to be, but I wanted to ensure the safety of another baby inside my womb.

The doctor performed a procedure in which he injected dye that caused my uterus, ovaries, and fallopian tubes to radiate while a low-dose X-ray machine took pictures. He checked for structural abnormalities that may have caused me to lose the baby in January. It was an awkward encounter to say the least. I laid on an exam table with my bottom half exposed. As he inflated a balloon-type device in my vagina, it caused too much pressure on my rectum, which made me soil myself. The two male doctors investigated my crotch as I lay in filth. In addition to the embarrassment, it hurt!

My doctor's head appeared from behind a secret curtain that blocked my view of the goings-on. "Everything appears healthy! I see no reason you can't try for another baby."

His words were both unnerving and exciting. We wanted another baby, but we were uneasy about my getting pregnant and possibly having the same thing happen again. We still didn't know the reason for the excessive bleeding that ultimately led to the demise of our last baby.

"So, there is nothing to indicate what the problem was last time?" I asked.

"The last one was just a fluke. Those situations are very rare. You are healthy, and it will probably be fine the next time."

I left, unsure and without the answer I was looking for. The decision to become pregnant again would require lots of dialogue and prayer between Cedric and me. Even through many counseling sessions, talks with friends and family, and prayers to God, I wasn't ready to be with child. My heart still needed some mending, and my soul needed to be fed. It had been running on empty.

To separate ourselves from our daily reality, we made a spontaneous decision to take our first-ever family vacation. I planned it only a couple of weeks prior to departure. We traveled across the country to Florida and soaked in the tropical paradise and Mickey Mouse for a week. It was temporary relief, but it was so much fun to escape that we decided to make it a yearly tradition.

☙❦❧

To stay mentally engaged the rest of the summer and keep my mind off pregnancy, I started reading a series of Christian fiction books about the end times; they consumed my every waking minute. I could not put them down! The possibility of being left on earth (without Jesus) to face harsh conditions beyond imagination scared me.

Am I going to heaven? I wondered. I hadn't exactly been a model Christian during the last few months. I'd pretty much folded when faced with my own personal trial. *Am I truly saved by the blood of Jesus Christ?*

Although the books were fiction, the underlying concepts were Biblical and too deep for my understanding. My church offered Bible studies, but I knew nothing about the Bible, compared to some of the people who attended. I felt too inferior to participate. I knew only the bare bones of the Bible: the traditional stories told to children in Sunday school. I had never delved into it much further than that. It intimidated me to go to a Bible study with more seasoned individuals, all of whom I considered much more faithful and wise than me.

I certainly had faith in God and believed in him, but my faith lacked one critical element, and that was trust. I didn't trust God with my earthly life. I really wanted to, though. It was necessary if I were to be serious about my relationship with him.

With much thought, contemplation, and hesitation, I worked up enough courage to attend my first small group study in the home of a lady whom I had always known to be a very strong and knowledgeable believer. The other ladies included three graduates of Christian high schools and colleges. They had married men from those backgrounds as well. One was the pastor's wife. The women had been raised in Christian homes, and some of their parents had been missionaries. In my childhood, my parents had taken me to church and prayed with me every night, but we were never as involved as these women were. I wanted to grow my faith in Christ. I brought certain inadequacies to the study, but I trusted the other ladies enough to help guide me through my spiritual quest.

The first thing I discovered was that a Bible study group required me to actually study. I hadn't done that since college, which was nearly six years earlier. I couldn't just rely on a video monologue given by a preacher to do the thinking for me. I had to read the Bible, think about it, and pray to God for discernment, because my prior attempts at Bible reading had left me muddled. It was vast, and certain parts had not been an easy read. Each week of Bible study gave me the opportunity to ask challenging questions and open up a dialogue with the more experienced women. Ultimately, they all came around to the same answers.

"Pray. He will reveal himself to you."

"The Bible is your guide. Read it, and then pray for understanding and discernment."

"Pray and then wait. He will open and close doors for you."

"God knows your heart. He will give you what you need, not what you want."

Easier said than done. I hated waiting. I was not a patient person. The women were wise, so I took what they said and kept it close to my heart. During the course of the study, I talked about the loss of my baby. The ladies often prayed over me for healing. They prayed about our decision whether to have another baby. The prayers always ended with "if it's God's will."

I hated that. God's will had obviously been different from my own in the last pregnancy. "God's will is the only will" seemed selfish. *That's it? A person accepts it or they don't? I can't change the outcome?* I found that truth difficult to understand. How could God allow so much pain? I believed what the Bible said about God being loving and good all of the time, but he had a strange way of showing it.

The simple fact was that I had to develop trust in him and trust that letting his will guide my life was far better than following my own. Single moments of temporary pain had to take a back seat to the greater good that God had in store. I had to let God lead me around until he provided me with a source of light that allowed me to see where I was going. That proved to be a difficult task. Too many times I tried to take control and failed to reach my intended outcome. It infuriated me to know God had the power to fix things, yet he didn't. He had possessed the power to save my baby. How could I trust him to do good when so much bad had happened? God could have easily given up on me, just as I almost gave up on him in the previous months of suffering.

Thankfully, he had an unconditional love that no one or nothing on earth could compete with. No baby could take his place, but I still felt empty without one.

seven

Taking the Plunge

The summer yielded a plethora of biblical knowledge. I achieved greater confidence in my relationship with God, although it remained a work in progress. Through much prayer and reading of scriptures, I felt armed and ready to take on challenges similar to those I had faced after losing Reece. Honestly, I didn't think anything like that would happen again. I figured I had done my time, and God would grant me clemency from any more hardships.

After petitioning to God about future pregnancies, I was left with no obvious answers. Cedric and I contemplated, each hoping the other might have had a vision or received some sort of message. We had nothing. We decided that if God wanted us to conceive a child, it would happen, so we made the emotional decision to try again. It had been almost eight months since our baby had died. I had received a clean bill of health. My spirit and hope had returned, for the most part. And the trauma of the loss had somewhat faded in our memories. It was surreal now to think about being pregnant and carrying another baby—replacing one we had lost—but we wanted another child.

We conceived immediately. We were overwhelmed with joy and knew God had blessed us. The pregnancy began exactly as the other one had. I had a touch of morning sickness and bouts of fatigue through the first trimester. School was back in session, and the work day exhausted me. There were times when I had to swivel my high-back chair away from the students and close my eyes for a few seconds. It was just enough to keep me from falling asleep in front of them.

Other than that, things were going smoothly. We even had enough confidence to take a vacation to Ohio with our daughter during Thanksgiving break. My doctor was not opposed, considering it was still early in the pregnancy, and I had not had any troubles.

My biggest concern was flying. Cedric was a pilot for an airline. He lived half of his life in the air. Regardless of his knowledge of air travel and his assurance of the airplane's structural integrity, I wasn't excited about our mode of transportation, because Cedric would not be flying our plane. However, his presence gave me some peace. At least he might be able to rush to the pilot's seat and take over if an emergency occurred. He had a knack for saving the day. I relied on his calm head to get through many days. He seemed to have a direct line to God too. His reliance on God for every little thing was a quality I hadn't acquired yet. It was definitely something I wanted.

Our three-day trip was chock-full of sightseeing, shopping, and a professional basketball game. Our time together provided memories for the family history book. The last evening, however, brought back a familiar foe. I started cramping. I tried to pass it off as the baby moving or my muscles stretching, but at thirteen weeks, I knew what was coming. I told Cedric about it, and all we could do was pray.

The old anger and resentment started to creep back in. I felt as if I had been betrayed by God again. The plane ride home was of little concern to me. I didn't care about anything going on around me. I sat in a trance, feeling trapped by the threat of another miscarriage. I knew it was a matter of weeks, or even days, until I started bleeding, and 2008 would end exactly as it had begun. I had no doubt.

I returned to school, despite constant cramping. It was unbearable at night. I frequently consulted Diane and updated her on my status. She was concerned but convinced me to keep working. "Bed rest didn't help you last time. God is in control. He has this."

I started bleeding on December 7, just as I had predicted a week earlier. For some reason, I was at peace and didn't worry about my physical well-being. After several appointments, my doctor still had no answers. The only positive feedback he gave me was that the baby and I were healthy. Several weeks passed, and the symptoms remained, despite persistent prayers and pleading to God.

࿇

Two days before Christmas, I received a disturbing phone call from a friend. Her infant daughter was very sick in the hospital with pneumonia. Everyone was greatly concerned. That evening I prayed for my friend and her child. It was the sort of prayer I had never considered before—I was normally too selfish—but something urged me to do it anyway. *God, please spare the life of my friend's baby. If it's your will, take my baby instead.*

Have I made a mistake? Did I really just ask God for that? What am I thinking? Another baby was something I had yearned for. Yet God answered before I had time to take back my words.

I started to have horrible cramping. To ease my pain, I curled up in the fetal position. I felt extreme pressure, and suddenly it burst, with a feeling of release. My pants were instantly soaked, but the cramping stopped. I went to the bathroom, and I expected to be covered in blood, but the moisture was clear. The bag of water surrounding the baby had broken.

I calmly informed Cedric, who had been in the other room. We piled into the car and drove to the hospital in silence. I was tormented with the thought that I had caused something to happen by curling my body in a position that put too much pressure on my womb. *Have I accidentally killed my baby?* I remained silent and never spoke of my actions. I disregarded the possibility that God had accomplished his will through my prayer. I blamed myself and planned to bear the burden for the rest of my life.

I called my mother and asked her to meet us at the hospital to get Kate. We were escorted to the labor and delivery floor, after a brief emergency room exam. The delivery of our sixteen-week-old baby was imminent. The charge nurse was extremely kind and sympathetic. She prepared the room and the bed just as they would in a normal delivery. I was able to move about and had no restrictions, except food and drink.

We had been at the hospital for less than an hour when I got up from bed to use the bathroom and felt pressure. The baby was coming. Cedric informed the nurse. Soon, I was surrounded by medical personnel. After one push, our baby boy was out on the bed. I smiled and felt his tiny head, which already had dark hair forming. He looked like a miniature version of a full-term baby. They swaddled his body and handed him to Cedric.

I never held him. I was having significant bleeding because the placenta would not release from my body. Surgery would be required to remove it. I had never had surgery or been put under anesthesia, so my anxiety level increased tenfold. I was very concerned about Kate, my only living child. *What if I don't wake up?*

Everything was a blur. The baby was taken to the nursery to be properly cleaned up. I was whisked out to the surgery room. I managed to squeak out, "Bye, Love" to my family.

I had an uneasy feeling right before being put under anesthesia. *What if these are my last thoughts?* Then I was out.

I don't know how long the surgery took or what happened during the procedure, but I woke up in a fog. My throat hurt from the breathing tube. I tried to talk but couldn't. I heard the nurse say that everything went well, and I would be going back to my room. I was ready to go home. It was December 23, and I had a lot to do before Christmas. I was determined not to have two failed Christmases in a row.

In the hospital room, I was confined to the bed, due to a medical balloon that had been inserted inside of me. It prevented excessive bleeding, which had been an issue during the surgery. I was instructed to massage my abdomen to get my uterus to contract and stop bleeding. The balloon was only temporary and would be removed in the evening. *Oh, goody.* I requested ice chips and wanted to be left alone.

Cedric returned to the room just after I arrived. He was visibly shaken.

"What's wrong?" I asked.

He choked up. "I said good-bye to our baby boy."

Seeing my husband bawling was too much for me. He lay on the bed with me, and we wept together. Once again, we left our baby to be discarded by the hospital personnel. I didn't know what happened to babies born prior to twenty weeks. I guess I didn't want to know. I knew families had the option of having a funeral or leaving the baby in the custody of the hospital. The thought of having to select a tiny casket made me ill. I wasn't ready to have a funeral for my child. It was terribly painful to consider, so we didn't. I assumed the grieving would be easier without having to go through that, but it wasn't.

I followed the doctor's orders and did my abdominal massage throughout the day. In the afternoon, I received an unexpected visitor. Linda, the pastor's wife from my Bible study group, dropped in. She happened to be a nurse on the labor and delivery floor. When I saw her, she began to cry. I tried to hold back my tears but was unsuccessful. Any time someone cried, I did the same. She gave me a hug.

"How did you know I was here?" I asked.

"I ran into a coworker at the store, and she mentioned a patient she'd cared for who had delivered a sixteen-week-old baby. I had a very strong feeling it was you."

Unfortunately, she had been correct. I knew she could feel my pain and sorrow, because she had also experienced two losses of her own. Luckily, she had an explanation for her failed pregnancies. Mine remained a mystery.

"We can put you on the prayer chain," she said.

"That would be greatly appreciated."

We said a quick prayer together, and she departed. I felt relieved that extra prayers were being said for us. Life was hard enough with prayers; I couldn't imagine what it was like without them.

I didn't have any more visitors, except doctors and nurses. Several came in at once to assist in removing the balloon that had been placed in me earlier. It was quick and painless, but one problem remained. I continued to bleed quite a lot. I massaged my abdomen harder and harder to stop the flow. The nurses stood back, conferring with one another to determine whether the doctor needed to be called in again, but something unexpected happened that immediately caused a frenzy. A giant mass of tissue protruded out of my vagina. The nurses freaked and started hollering all at once.

"Call the doctor, call the doctor, now!"

Uh, oh, that isn't reassuring, I thought.

"Stop massaging!"

"What is it?" I asked.

"I don't know!"

I panicked. "What is it? What is it? What is going on?" I yelled repeatedly.

There was mass hysteria. Cedric tried to calm me down, but the nurses' alarm spread to me. The doctor rushed in seconds later, though it seemed like hours. He took one look and said, "Oh, I guess I didn't get all of the placenta during surgery. I didn't want to scar your uterus by scraping it too hard, so I wasn't aggressive with the instrument. Give me one push, and it will come out."

That did it. Once the softball-size piece of placenta was out, my bleeding slowed dramatically.

There was never a dull moment during my hospital stays. I remained overnight and was released the morning of Christmas Eve. We left with a small box filled with keepsakes to memorialize our baby. It was all we had of our baby boy whom we named Izzy (short for Isaiah). Only a tiny box represented a human life. There was nothing else—no memories, milestone pictures, drawings by little hands, report cards, or trophies.

We observed another Christmas with empty arms and broken hearts. Our grief was immeasurable, and mine was compounded by the hidden guilt that I might have caused the baby's death. Only one thing differed from the last experience. This time I relied on faith and God's everlasting love to carry me through the storm. I couldn't let my family experience another year of having an absent wife and mother. Life did not stop, because I was not ready to move forward. That was the crux of it. It kept going, with or without me. I wanted to be faithful and continue on God's path, despite difficulties along the way.

❧

In late January 2009, we received the medical reports from the laboratory that had tested for problems with our baby and my placenta. That was a normal procedure following miscarriages. The report read, "PRODUCTS OF CONCEPTION, NORMAL & INTACT."

That statement enraged me. *How dare they call my baby a product, as if he was some item at the grocery store! He was a human being. How can the people writing these reports have souls?*

The report offered me no peace. There was still no reason or explanation for my losses. I stared at a seemingly blank piece of paper that presented no solutions. I considered that maybe it was God's way of telling me to be patient or perhaps to give up. My having another baby didn't seem to be part of God's plan. It appeared that we needed to close that chapter of our lives, but I didn't know for sure, due to the unknown cause of my problematic pregnancies.

It also saddened me too much to consider that my child-bearing days might be over. I wanted a logical reason before quitting. The mystery behind God's will drove me insane.

eight

One Last Try

I pressed on through the spring of 2009 while fighting off the anxiety demons that kept trying to creep back into my life. With much spiritual exercise on my knees and physical exercise on the treadmill, I stayed focused and successfully completed the school year without having a nervous breakdown.

In a vain attempt to make up for our second loss, Cedric and I decided to take our daughter on a family vacation to Hawaii the week before Memorial Day. My sister's family and our mother joined us. We determined that it would be a fantastic distraction from real life and a chance to focus on Kate and spoil her rotten. We surfed the powerful ocean waves, trekked across an active volcano, snorkeled with all sorts of wild creatures, and watched our daughter learn Polynesian dances. She seemed to be our miracle baby, and we made once-in-a-lifetime memories with her.

After the vacation, it was back to business. I needed quick answers regarding my failed pregnancies. I was twenty-nine and feeling pressure to figure out my pregnancy issues before my body decided it was too old to bear children. I spent the summer researching on the Internet, consulting with specialists, and giving enough blood to the labs to fill up a gallon jug. Test after test came back normal. Anyone with a real health problem would have been thrilled, but I was not so enthused.

"I am stumped," said my new doctor, a perinatologist specializing in high-risk pregnancies. "If you decide to get pregnant again, we can try a few things. The way things have gone, I am not sure they will work. These pregnancies were not flukes, but I just have no answers."

He was the best doctor in his field. People from surrounding states traveled long distances to see him for treatment. I trusted his judgment. I was completely taken aback when he said, "We will hope and pray that this will work out for you."

He was doing everything in his power to help me, but even he acknowledged his limitations. Cedric and I took his advice and prayed constantly. We asked the most spiritual people we knew to pray that God would open or shut the door permanently. We had to have a clear answer from him. Month after month, we prayed but felt no leading. It was quite discouraging. We sought God with everything we had, and we didn't receive any message in return. The prospects of having another baby seemed to dwindle. There were no answers coming from any direction.

❧❦

Fall brought another new school year and provided a pleasant distraction from my baby fever. I did ponder pregnancy occasionally, due to the fact that another coworker was pregnant; however, I fell into the rhythm of work, and the semester passed in a blur.

December marked one year since we had lost Izzy. We made a daring choice to try to conceive one last time. If we succeeded, we would consider it an open door. If we didn't, we would know God was closing it.

The winter never failed to be a season of baby drama. Once again, this proved true. We conceived right away and felt that it was a blessing from God because of our perseverance in seeking his will. We truly believed this baby was the one who would survive. We were finally going to be parents to another baby.

We shared the news immediately with our friends and family so that they could start praying for the little miracle inside me. I felt the best I had in almost two years. It was finally my turn. God wouldn't let me down this time. I continued to see the perinatologist, and he prescribed a regimen of antibiotics and aspirin. It was a normal combination for what he suspected my previous pregnancy issue had been: blood clots behind the placenta was his best guess. He offered us little reassurance, considering that he had no official diagnosis.

"One day at a time," he said. "I think things will be good this time."

I wholeheartedly agreed. After all, I had rededicated myself to serve God in a more fruitful way. I was doing all I possibly could to please him. I read scriptures each night, prayed many times a day, and attended more Bible studies and church activities.

I visited my perinatologist and my regular obstetrician (OB) every two weeks and watched my baby grow perfectly in every way. The most stressful part of the pregnancy, the thirteenth week, was fast approaching. That was when all hell had broken loose with the last two pregnancies. I could feel every muscle in my body tense up each time I used the restroom. I held my breath and would slowly look down at the toilet paper. I expected the worst, but there was nothing—all clear. I had only occasional mild cramping that seemed like normal pregnancy aches and pains.

The thirteenth and fourteenth weeks passed uneventfully. I relaxed and believed I was home free. I praised the Lord and smiled again and again. Life was good.

The fifteenth week of the pregnancy coincided with spring break. Birds were singing, everything was green, flowers blossomed, and we enjoyed being outdoors after a long winter's hibernation. Everything around us seemed brighter and fresher than it had in the past. The storm clouds were gone, and sunshine took their place. The pain we had experienced from the previous losses vanished, and nothing but joy remained. We were so thankful. Little did we know, God had trained us so that we would be ready to face our most difficult task yet.

March 14, 2010, marked the start of a marathon race that would end in victory for one of us and teach the rest about perseverance, sacrifice, and love. For the third time, my body decided that it didn't like being pregnant. Just as in the second miscarriage, cramping preceded a gush of blood-stained fluid from my womb. Amniotic fluid, as I had learned, was critical for the health of the baby. The fluid cushioned the baby and helped him learn how to breathe. Each drop was crucial to help develop strong lungs.

I went to the hospital to get checked. The ultrasound revealed that some fluid was left, but a lot had been lost. I was told to drink as much water as possible to try to replenish the amniotic fluid. I was also prescribed rest because I would most likely go into preterm labor sooner, rather than later. The baby was still alive but at risk, and I was at risk of developing certain infections that were resistant to antibiotics. In addition, there was a chance of heavy bleeding because I was taking aspirin.

All that I cared about was the baby's survival. I called everyone I could to tell them about the situation, requested their prayers, and asked them to inform everyone they knew to pray. Medicine and science had failed again. All that we had left was prayer. Based on my history, we would need a miracle.

I drank gallons of water daily. I hated it, but if it would save my baby, I was all for it. I relieved myself two or three times an hour, but it was very difficult doing that at work. I had to page Diane to cover my classes so that I could use the restroom.

Despite the constant fluid loss, I hoped at each doctor's appointment that the baby would be surrounded by lifesaving liquid. Both the perinatologist and the OB took ultrasound pictures at every angle possible to find any pocket of fluid, but little was found. They each ended the appointments by saying something like, "Keep praying. . . . Keep doing what you're doing. The baby is hanging on. . . . Usually, women go into labor with so little fluid. He is hanging on for a reason."

We were having another boy: a son to play in the dirt, shoot baskets, and fly to the moon. We made it longer than expected, so we had beat one set of odds. There was still hope.

Weeks went by, and our baby boy stayed put. I continued to lose fluid, and the bleeding got heavier. Work became exceedingly difficult, because I was in the restroom or at the doctor's office more than in the classroom.

"I will admit you to the hospital at twenty-four weeks," said my doctor. "At that point the baby could live outside the womb. Usually, a baby at that gestational age has about a 10 percent chance of survival. However, your baby's odds may be lower due to being in the womb without enough amniotic fluid.

"It's better than nothing." I trembled at the thought of a lengthy hospital stay, but the baby was my number-one priority. I would have to wait it out two more weeks.

God, let this baby live, I prayed.

Waiting was torturous. One particular day at school I was fed up with my frequent bathroom trips to take care of my body, which was being drained of blood and other fluids. Frustration took over. I called Diane from my desk and told her to meet me in the restroom. She sent a substitute to my room, and I left in tears. The mental and emotional exhaustion of another bad pregnancy had caught up with me. As we entered the private bathroom, I lost it.

"I am tired of this! Why is God doing this to me again?"

I desperately wanted answers from anyone, but none could be offered—even from my best friends.

Diane consoled me with a hug and said, "I don't know the reason. All I know is this is the last time you have to do this. You made it further this time than you did with the others. God has a reason, and he doesn't have to explain it to us, because he is God."

I managed to straighten myself up for the last hour of the school day, but I left worn out.

My frustration carried over to my family and God. The twenty-four-week point was days away, and I didn't want to leave my home. The hospital I was going to stay in was two hours away. It was logistically impossible for my husband and daughter to visit often. I had lost so much, and separation from my loved ones added to the pain. I wanted everyone to feel what I felt emotionally and bear the same burden I did, but it was impossible. I was jealous for their lives, which were unimpeded by suffering. I wanted to yell, "Everyone, stop what you are doing! Experience what I am feeling! Suffer with me!"

As for God, I was perplexed about the path he had chosen for me. I had no idea what he wanted from me. *What are you teaching me*, I asked, *and why does the lesson have to be learned this way?*

I felt like Job from the Old Testament. He had lost everything but remained faithful. Because of his faithfulness, he reaped more than he had before. I was motivated by that. I fought the urge to give up on God; it would get me nowhere. I thought if I persevered and remained faithful, God would reward me with a baby who lived. Being in a hospital, away from my loved ones, and trying to save a baby who had less than a 10 percent chance of surviving would be the ultimate test of my faith.

nine

Changes

Life completely changed for us in the month of May. We sold our house and bought my parents'—the one I had lived in during my youth. My mother had been widowed for four years and decided it was too big for her. We considered it the perfect house to raise our growing family in. I had made lots of memories in it as a child and wanted my children to have the same opportunity.

I decided to quit my teaching job at the end of the semester and take a different one, closer to our new home. I wouldn't start it until after our son's arrival, which was anticipated to be September 5. Everything fell into place. It seemed as if despite my trial, God had brought lots of positive changes into our lives. It gave me hope that we would also be blessed with a healthy baby.

The last day of the 2009–2010 school year marked exactly twenty-four weeks into my pregnancy. I finished grading tests, straightened up my room, packed my personal effects, and turned in my grade book for the final time. I hugged Diane, and we said our good-byes. I wasn't sure how often I would see her. She was a face I would miss.

I had packed my clothing the night before, in preparation for my extended stay at the hospital. My family met me at the school, and we set off for our destination, which was somewhat unknown. I prayed that the end result would be worth the sacrifice of abandoning all that I knew.

The drive seemed much longer than two hours. The miles and miles of golden wheat waved as we drove between the tiny towns that dotted the highway. In Oklahoma, the wheat that had grown through the winter was nearly ripe and would be harvested in June. Crews were readying their combines, tractors, and grain carts in preparation for the upcoming harvest. The countryside would look much different whenever the time came for me to return home in the fall. The wheat would be long gone, and the brown barren soil would be exposed.

I wondered what kind of changes I would experience by that time. With each mile, I grew more anxious. The car closed in on me; it suffocated me. I rolled down the window to get some air into my lungs. On the horizon, I could see a huge cross atop the hospital: my new home. I remained focused on the cross. It rotated and seemed to follow us as we drove along the highway parallel to it. The name of the hospital was Mercy. Both the symbol and the name seemed fitting for the situation I faced, but I wouldn't truly understand sacrifice and mercy until further into the future.

My first stop was to see my doctor in his office. He did a quick scan and asked if I was ready to go.

"Absolutely! If it gives us any chance at all, absolutely."

Within minutes, a nurse was wheeling me down a long private corridor that connected the physicians' offices to the hospital. It was eerily quiet. Along the way, I glanced at walls filled with crosses, portraits depicting Bible stories, and scriptures of hope. All were strategically placed so as to gain the most attention by the weary souls escorted to the hospital for one reason or another. On one hand, it was very peaceful, but on the other, it was unsettling.

The corridor terminated in a bank of elevators. We ascended to the fifth floor. It housed women with troubled pregnancies, as well as the neonatal intensive care unit (NICU), where premature and sick babies were cared for. The fifth floor was affectionately known as the troublemaker floor. If a woman had pregnancy issues, it was the place to be. It provided the best hospital care for mothers and premature infants. After a few turns—right, left, right—we were at the security doors. Once inside, the nurse wheeled me down another hallway toward my room. As I passed the other rooms, I could hear the sounds of heartbeats. It was very familiar; they were babies' heartbeats being monitored. Each room contained a woman desperately hoping her sacrifice had paid off, and that she and her baby would be survivors, overcomers. Each woman waited for it to be her turn to be a new mother.

While my nurse retrieved my paperwork, I sat at the threshold of my room and pondered. I knew our lives were certain to be different, but how different remained to be seen. All I knew was that I had done everything in my power to give my son a chance to live. I had been a good mommy. His fate would be determined by God. My deep thoughts were interrupted by the nurse.

"This is where you'll be staying until the baby is born. If you are here long enough, we could switch you to the other side of the hall for a different view. The golf course is over there."

"Thanks." *I guess.*

My first house-warming gift was a steroid shot in the rump. "This is going to burn a little," said the nurse.

"Thank you for the warning. Ow! Good Lord, that hurts!"

"Sorry. It's a necessary evil. The steroid will help develop the baby's lungs more quickly in the event of an early arrival."

Evening soon fell upon us, and Cedric had to leave to care for our daughter. Of course, I bawled and wanted him to stay, but I knew it wasn't possible. I had some comfort knowing I was in a safe place. I sat alone on my bed for the remainder of the evening and cried through each bite of cafeteria parmesan chicken, which later gave me a severe case of heartburn. *What a nice welcome.*

∽∾

Life on the fifth floor was anything but glamorous. Monitors, IVs, and other medical devices littered the room. An old tube TV adorned a corner of the ceiling. Spiritual pictures hung on the walls, covering the cold white paint. A window provided a view of the busy highway and the hospital parking lot. Both were gray and absent of soulful colors that elicited any emotional response except gloominess. The bed was like a deflated air mattress. It was designed to automatically adjust pressure to reduce the chance of bed sores. I would never use *comfortable* to describe my situation.

The continuous barrage of nurses who came in to monitor the baby and me got tiresome. Two belts that recorded the baby's heartbeat and my contractions were my latest fashion accessories. Multiple times a day and night, a squirt of jelly and the blue belts that firmly squeezed my abdomen became part of my routine. The nurses did it so frequently I was able to do it myself anytime I wanted so that I could hear the sweet sounds of my son's heartbeat. Faced with odds not in our favor, I felt a surreal joy to hear each beat.

My doctor made occasional visits but never really checked anything. He would sit down and talk like a friend. Before leaving, he always said, "You have amazed me. Keep doing whatever you're doing. I didn't think you would make it this far."

Aside from that, it was fear and loneliness that kept me company. The TV had minimal channels. It played soap operas by day and criminal shows in the evening that left me with nightmares.

I had brought along a box of craft supplies, so that I could make something each week for my daughter. Those were met with mixed reviews. She never acted thrilled to be there visiting, and that didn't help my morale. However, her visit each week meant an outdoor jaunt in the wheelchair. The doctor was kind enough to free me from my cell and allowed me time outside for good behavior—that is, good vitals from the baby and me. The fifteen minutes of fresh air and sunlight renewed my hope of surviving in my cage, but the hurt returned each time my family left. I missed them and the normal-ish life we had before the pregnancy. I held back my tears until I could see Cedric and Kate in the parking lot. I refused to let anyone think of me as frail and unable to endure the challenge God had placed before me.

Every time I looked out the window, it was like looking into another world. Time seemed to stand still in the hospital, but everything else on the outside carried on. Cars came and went, patients left to go home, and the sun continued to rise and fall. With each passing day, my mental health was in jeopardy and my physical body fared worse. I lost copious amounts of blood and amniotic fluid daily. I was being pumped full of steroids to develop the baby's lungs, IV fluids to stay hydrated, electrolytes to keep my internal systems balanced, and antibiotics to stave off infections. Things were stable but unstable.

Every part of me was failing, except my spiritual walk with God. I prayed continuously for a miracle. I read the Bible constantly. I contacted strangers on the Internet from all over the United States to join me in prayer. I gave

everything I had. I was unsure of the result of my perseverance, but I could not and would not give up on God and
his power. The unknown was whether his will and my will
were aligned.

Three weeks of supplication, asking, and pouring out
my soul to God was my breaking point. June 4, 2010, marked
the heaviest, most gruesome bleeding since the pregnancy
had begun. Huge clots of blood and pieces of amniotic sac
made their way out of my body. I had carried my son twenty-
seven weeks. I was weary, afraid, and dejected. I cried out to
God, "Stop this! Stop this!"

I called the nurses to let them know about the clots and
the sac pieces. They called the doctor. "He said no food or
drink. He'll be here to check you soon."

I was hooked up to the monitors and having strong
contractions. Ironically, I couldn't feel them at all. I could
only think it was God burdening himself with my physical
anguish. Blood was drawn to make sure of my blood type,
in the event a transfusion was needed. A sense of urgency
filled my room.

I knew the circumstances that day were different. The
perinatologist, the anesthesiologist, and the neonatologist
formed our team. My doctor watched the monitors carefully for several minutes. He reviewed the paper that had
recorded the contractions from the past hour. The monitor
revealed that the baby's heart rate was decelerating during
the contractions. It was a sign that the baby was in distress.

"We need to deliver you very soon," he said. "The baby
doesn't need any more stress, and neither does your body.

I'm afraid the day's disruption is due to an infection in your uterus. No antibiotic can fix it. You are both at risk of being very sick or even dying if we don't deliver."

We had run out of time and options. Our baby boy was coming into the world. I was overwhelmed with sentiment. I had been able to keep him safe for so long, but I knew my role was switching from my baby's keeper to a cheerleader, encouraging him to fight and shouting to God for a miracle.

I called my husband to tell him to come to the hospital immediately. He had a two-hour drive; there was nothing immediate about that. Very strong antibiotics were administered through the IV, and I continued to be monitored closely. My doctor needed to perform a C-section for a speedier delivery and to minimize the stress on the baby. Cedric arrived as the doctor explained the surgery.

"You will receive a spinal block that will numb you from the bottom of your ribcage down to your toes. I'll make a small incision just above your pubic bone. The baby will be removed and handed to the neonatology team that is stationed in the room."

"So, today is definitely the day?" Cedric asked.

"Oh, yes. We have to do this now. I worry she may have an infection that is causing her body to go into labor. It's basically the body's way of saying something is wrong."

"It's so early. What about the baby?"

"The neonatologist will explain what they will do to help the baby. She will be in later. I'll see you both soon."

There wasn't even enough time to think. The anesthesiologist came in to explain the spinal block in greater detail, and the neonatologist arrived soon after that, with matter-of-fact news.

"Your baby is very early. Because he hasn't had fluid to develop his lungs, he will likely be very sick. We won't know for sure until we have him here to assess. The odds are not good; I am sure you know this. I will do all I can to help him. Pray for a miracle."

As she exited, we caught our breath and prayed. We could do nothing more. Surgery, infection, a sick baby, and poor odds didn't make for a joyful prayer. God's will was being done; we just accepted it.

ten

His Perfection

When my bed was rolled to the surgery room, it was like entering onto a stage where I was to perform. I lay in a not-so-modest position with tubes and IVs coming and going out of me. The lights on the ceiling were like spotlights and just as blinding. My audience consisted of three doctors, eight nurses, and a nervous husband. The star of the drama was soon to be born.

Please let him be okay, I prayed.

"Can you feel that?" asked my doctor, as he tested the effectiveness of the spinal block.

"Feel what?" I stammered. I was so nervous; my body was visibly trembling.

"Are you okay?" asked the anesthesiologist, who was standing near my head.

"Yeah, I'm just freaked out right now."

"I'm watching you closely. Your vitals look great," he said, gently rubbing my shoulder for reassurance.

A curtain blocked my view, so I couldn't see what my doctor was doing to the lower part of my body.

"Wow," he said. "You are the skinniest patient I have worked on. You have hardly any fat."

What? I could feel pressure and pulling on my abdomen.

"Almost there," he said. It seemed as if I had lain there for hours, but I had been in the operating room only about twenty minutes.

Then suddenly he hollered, "He's here!"

I heard our two-pound, ten-ounce baby boy, Samuel, make one joyful scream. It was heavenly. The doctor held him up so that I could see while Cedric cut the umbilical cord. Samuel was whisked over to the incubator so that the neonatologist could assess his condition.

"He's perfect. He is going to be fine. It's a miracle," said my husband.

I couldn't see my son, and I didn't hear any more crying from him. The nurse pushed his bed beside mine so that I could look at him. His head was turned, and his eyes were open, looking directly at me. He appeared to squirm like a normal baby.

"We are taking the baby to the NICU so we can stabilize things. You can see him once the doctor gets you fixed up," the nurse said.

I had forgotten that my gut lay open and needed to be closed up. My attention was on my son and his well-being. Part of the nightmare was finally over. I wouldn't be dealing with any more fluids gushing from my body. Once I was stitched up, and the tools and the gauze were accounted for, my doctor leaned over and stroked my forehead. "You did great."

I managed a weak smile. Cedric gave him a hug and thanked him for his extraordinary care and efforts.

I was greeted by my pastor and his wife in my regular room. Other friends and family members were there as well. We updated them with all that we knew; it wasn't much. Cedric was much more optimistic than I. I was still numb, physically and also emotionally. I didn't want to hope too much, so I remained guarded.

The neonatologist called while everyone was in the room and updated us. "We are trying a couple of different things to help your baby breathe. His lungs are not working well."

My vision blurred as my eyes welled with tears. A fog came over my mind as sorrow filled my heart. My intuition told me our baby wasn't going to make it. The spinal block wore off from the surgery, and my abdomen burned. I received morphine to ease the pain. I instantly felt drunk, but the pain remained. I was in and out of a stupor. I regained my senses once the effects of the morphine faded, but then the pain was too intense to even think straight. I was given more of the drug. I wished it was to deaden the pain of knowing my baby was dying, rather than to reduce the physical pain.

అా⬦

By midnight, everyone was gone. It was just Cedric and me, waiting to get word from the doctor. Hour after hour ticked away, then finally the phone rang. It was the neonatologist with another update.

"We are doing everything, and nothing is working. You need to come see your baby now."

I hung up the phone and explained to Cedric what the doctor had said. We both began weeping. It hurt me physically to cry; the pain was unbearable. Every heave felt as if I was ripping my abdomen open. The nurse brought me a wheelchair. Moving from the bed to the chair caused me to cry out in pain. With a nurse escort, Cedric wheeled me to the NICU, where our son lay perfectly still in an incubator. He was covered in tubes and sensors that monitored his failing vitals.

We took a few pictures and gave the nurse the camera and told her to take some for us. From my wheelchair, I reached out to put my finger in Samuel's tiny hand. There was no movement. I prayed at that moment that he would clench my finger so he'd know I was with him. His body remained motionless. Beeps and buzzers sounded all around us and indicated low levels of everything. All were signs our son was slipping away. The machines did all of the work for him, but even they couldn't maintain normal vitals. He hadn't breathed on his own since his one and only cry in the operating room. He hadn't opened his eyes since he'd looked at me before being taken away. Perhaps that was his good-bye to me.

The nurse removed some of the tubes so that we could hold Samuel. There was an eerie calm in the room. Oddly, I felt at peace. The overwhelming sadness that had consumed me minutes earlier was temporarily absent, and joy filled my heart. The monitors were silenced. I was the first to hold him. I kissed his head and caressed his dark brown hair. I touched each finger on each hand and did the same with his toes and feet. Each part of him was perfect. He was another example of God's awesome design. Our boy had been placed in the world for a reason. God made no mistakes.

As Cedric held his son, I sat back and observed a father bond with his boy. I imagined them playing with tractors and four-wheelers and fishing off our dock. I imagined a father showing his son how to be a Christian man.

I glanced back at the heart monitor that showed the rate of our son's slowing heart—8, 7, 6, 5, 4, 3, 2, 1, 0.

I squeezed Cedric's arm and whispered, "He's gone."

We had our much-yearned-for baby for nine treasured hours. With one final caress of his forehead, we left our son in the room, but he wasn't alone. We left a part of our hearts with him, and more important, God remained there with open arms, waiting to receive his child into the gates of heaven.

ॐॐ

As I lay in the hospital bed with Cedric by my side, I was unable to sleep. My head was bombarded by many thoughts. Strangely, they didn't seem to be coming from me. My inner voice was corrupt from too much grief to produce such spiritually meaningful words about my son. The voice speaking was bold and strong, yet peaceful—it was heaven-ly. I could not make sense of what was going on. I grabbed the journal I had started in the hospital and used a flash-light so that I could scribble what was pinging around in my brain. It was as if someone was doing the thinking and writing for me, as my hand scrolled each word effortlessly across the page.

> Samuel Reith Janzen, you had people praying to God more than they ever had in their entire lives. You taught people to love and value each other. You softened the hearts of strangers and non-believers. Grown men wept for you. You provided happi-ness. You brought our family closer together. You showed us we need to fight for the weak, regardless of the outcome. People grew closer to God because of you.

The thoughts combined to create a picture of how God had wanted me to live all along. I needed to live with a greater love for God and his people. Samuel's purpose had been to deliver God's message. Even a tiny, unknown human could spread his word. Samuel had served God, and he served him to perfection. He was only with us a few hours but left an everlasting impression on our hearts. The moments spent with Samuel that night were our last. We chose to have him cremated and have a memorial at a later date.

My doctor came for one final visit on June 6, the day after Samuel died.

"Are you ready to leave?" he asked.

The question caught me off guard, because I'd just had surgery a day and a half before that. "You'll let me go?"

"Yeah. You need to go home. You've been here way too long and gone through way too much. Normally, I'd keep you. Your insurance covers you for a few more days as well. But I think it's best for you to go. I'm sorry this didn't work out."

He checked my sutures, gave me a hug, and left. I was finally free to go. Ironically, I didn't want to. The life that I knew before was gone—my old house, my old job, my baby. I didn't want to have to start over. I wanted everything to remain the same.

The drive home that hot June afternoon was filled with tears. Some were from grief, and others were from a fear of change. As we drove past the empty wheat fields, I couldn't help but feel the same as their current state. I, too, had been stripped of my seed that I'd spent months sustaining, and all that remained was a hollow shell, which was never to be used again.

❧❦

The next few weeks were an emotional typhoon. I was still in pain from the surgery, so that did not help my attitude. I cried. I laughed. I raged. The littlest thing would set me off. My mother, my daughter, and I got pedicures, and as we walked through a department store my daughter stepped on my toe, smearing the polish. I was livid. I screamed at her and then broke down crying hysterically about my marred pedicure.

"It's okay. We can go back, and they will fix it," my mom said.

"Everything is always screwed up for me," I said, in between sobs.

I had postpartum depression, combined with various stages of grief. I wasn't much fun to be around. In general, I avoided people. I didn't want to answer questions or embarrass myself with another crying fit. I took a sabbatical from pretty much all routine activities, such as church, grocery shopping, and visiting friends. My physical wounds and emotional ones needed time to heal.

Thankfully, it was summertime. I sat outside a lot with my eyes closed and my mind drifting with the warm breeze. I never doubted God's sovereign power and his ability to bring me through my trial. I certainly didn't know why he had chosen me to endure it, but I'd figured out long ago that God didn't always give answers when I wanted them or the way I wanted them.

I mulled over my journal many times, hoping to make better sense of why things happened. I felt a nudging to share my thoughts with other people, but I wasn't ready to. They were too personal. I truly believed they were inspired by God, so I figured I should remain humble by keeping them to myself. The nudging continued, and I wasn't sure how to handle that. I considered that maybe it was God wanting me to share those intimate details of my journal.

I boldly contacted my pastor and asked about having a memorial service during church on Samuel's actual due date, September 5. I wanted to be the one speaking about Samuel, so I requested to do the sermon.

"I sort of have an idea what the sermon will be about."

"That sounds great," he said.

That was too easy, I thought.

It made me nervous to think about delivering a message from God to other people. I had never done that. I was not even remotely comfortable praying short prayers aloud in front of other people whose heads were bowed and eyes closed, let alone speaking for a half hour with all eyes focused on me. I didn't know exactly what I would say to honor God and Samuel at the same time.

I had about one and a half months to get a sermon together. Fortunately, God had been working on that for me.

eleven

Open Doors

Though still grieving, we decided to keep with tradition and take our annual family vacation to Florida. I hadn't planned it, because I'd anticipated being in the hospital, pregnant with Samuel the entire summer. We were going to wing it. Before leaving, I had one last appointment with my perinatologist to be medically cleared for travel.

"How are you doing?" he asked.

"Pretty good," I said. "There are good days and bad days."

"That's expected. You have gone through a major ordeal that most people will never encounter. I'm sorry it didn't work out."

"I appreciate that. We are grateful to have had you as a doctor. Thank you for everything."

"I wish we could figure out what the deal is with you," he said. "If you do consider pregnancy again, we'll try a couple of different things to see if it helps."

"Unfortunately, I'm done. It's just not meant to be," I said, holding back tears. It pained me to say those words. They were so final, much like death, but death would have been easier than admitting defeat.

"I understand," said my doctor. "I don't blame you."

He exchanged hugs with Cedric and me, and we parted ways. I was so sad, because I really felt as if he'd become our friend and advocate. I realized we would probably never cross paths with him again.

I spent the weekend packing, begrudgingly. I wasn't in the mood to visit the happiest place on earth. We had visited Disney World and several other Florida attractions in the past. In fact, we'd enjoyed it so much the first time, it had become a yearly getaway. Yet the previous visits had been under happier circumstances. We had one primary goal for our trip in 2010, and that was to spread some of Samuel's ashes.

On Sunday, July 25, the day before leaving, I received a phone call from Diane while we drove home after lunch with my mother.

"What are you up to?" she asked. She had such giddiness in her voice; I couldn't help but feel happy.

"Well, we're getting ready to go on vacation tomorrow."

"That sounds like fun! Where are you headed?"

"Florida. We're taking some of Samuel's ashes with us to leave behind," I said. "We plan to deposit his ashes in one of our favorite photo spots. The location is a secret, because I'm afraid a crazy mouse and his uniformed friends will come after us."

"That is awesome," she said. "I wanted to tell you something important. It's good you are going on vacation, because you can ponder it while you are away."

"Okay. What is it?" I asked.

"I was at my great-nephew Jace's first birthday party yesterday," Diane said. "My niece, Kourtney, was scooping ice cream and told a family member that she wanted to have a baby for a couple who has had trouble with pregnancy. She wants to be a surrogate. At first, she mentioned carrying a baby for a relative who had fertility issues, but they were already in the process of adopting a child. So, I told her about you guys. She really wants to help someone. You guys would be perfect. You deserve a baby. She wants to meet you soon. Maybe you all could meet at my house on neutral ground. She only lives twenty minutes away from you. Enjoy your vacation, give this some thought, and let me know."

"Uh, thanks. Bye," I said.

I had no words. *What just happened? A stranger who lives nearby wants to have my baby.* Astonished by Diane's proposal, I sat in the passenger seat of the car with my mouth agape.

Cedric startled me. "Hey! Who was that?"

"That was Diane," I mumbled while still processing what she had said.

"What did she want?"

"She called to tell me she has a niece who wants to be a surrogate. She lives twenty minutes from us. Diane mentioned us to her." *Maybe this is the divine intervention we have been looking for.*

Cedric shook his head in confusion. "Wow! That is interesting. Okay."

"I know, right?"

Neither of us knew what to do—or even say, for that matter. The only thing I knew about surrogacy was a vague definition. It wasn't a concept that I'd ever thought seriously about. I had seen an occasional movie or news story where one woman carried another woman's baby. We were adjusting to our life with only one child. It was apparent that was all God wanted us to have. What was the surrogacy thing all about? God was always up to something that I rarely understood, but he mystified me all the more by throwing surrogacy onto our laps.

I wanted to meet Diane's niece badly, but despite the strange and intriguing news, we had a quest to fulfill in Florida: laying our son to rest. Our trips to Florida had begun after the death of our second child in 2008, and we'd visited twice in 2009. The vacations allowed us a temporary reprieve from our grief. It was only for a week, but that was time we focused on the three of us and formed closer bonds. Our vacations became part of our family's identity.

We carefully sealed Samuel's ashes in a small plastic vial and placed it in our carry-on luggage. We guarded the bag on our flight as if it were filled with jewels. Once we settled in at our hotel, Cedric secured the vial in his pocket, and we set off in the evening to our favorite photo spot, where we had gotten our picture taken during each of our Florida vacations. It was a great reminder for us to see how we had changed from year to year.

I had read that depositing human ashes was frowned on in certain places. I served as the criminal mastermind and had everything planned so that we would avoid getting caught. It was a tricky undertaking, because there were eyes in the sky, the ground, the lampposts, and probably even the french fries. The area was heavily guarded with various . . . ahem . . . characters.

I untied my five-year-old decoy's shoe and sent her to the fence for a photo-op. I asked the paid photographer if I could take a picture with my own camera. She gave me the go-ahead nod, so I began snapping away and directing Kate to the best spot that would conceal the "drop-off."

Soon it was Cedric's and my turn to move in. I created a diversion. "Oh, her shoe is untied. Stay there, Kate. I don't want you to trip. I'll come tie your shoes."

We made a commotion as we stooped to tie her shoe. Cedric talked loudly, and I slid my camera across the ground. (Yes, it was scratched.) Cedric had the vial in one hand nearest the wrought-iron fence that enclosed the land forbidden to guests. As I tied Kate's shoe, Cedric looked around, reached through the fence, and sprinkled Samuel's ashes.

We looked at each other with moist eyes. We grinned and hugged Kate. To top off our caper, we asked the unassuming photographer, who had been mesmerized by the glow of the fireworks, to take our picture. Unbeknownst to her, Samuel was included.

Was what we did that evening unorthodox? Yes. Sneaky? Yes. Illegal? Probably. However, individuals really don't know what they are capable of until they have been tested.

❧

After a week's worth of Florida sun and much contemplation about God's will, we anticipated meeting the mystery woman who might have given us a reason to hope. I called Diane so that she could set up a blind date at her house. August 4, a few days after returning from vacation, we were going to meet Kourtney—a possible angel sent to us.

I anxiously waited for the day to come, but I feared rejection. What if she didn't like the looks of us? What if we hated her? What if she were to change her mind? It was certain to open up a wound that was still healing. I prayed that God would provide us with a unique opportunity to be parents again.

At 3:00 p.m. on the 4th, two women walked through a door into an unexplored world. Neither Kourtney nor I knew what we were doing, what we were getting into, or where the path would lead us. It was like a page from C. S. Lewis's Narnia series. It was sure to be an interesting, almost unbelievable adventure if it came to fruition.

Kourtney entered Diane's house with a warm smile, bright blue eyes, and arms extended. We hugged as Diane introduced us to one another. It was more than just a friendly exchange. The embrace was symbolic, in that there was sympathy on her part and much gratitude on mine. We quickly got past the formal introductions and jumped right into talking about families, careers, and hometowns. They were the standard conversation openers, but I didn't really think blurting out, "Will you have my baby? Please, please, please!" would appeal to her.

Eventually, we did get around to the topic of pregnancy, including my failures and her successes. I wanted her to know every detail, so that she would understand the long suffering of a mother who yearned for a child. I wanted her to feel the heartache of a mother who had lost a child. I wanted to make sure she knew that no matter what the age of a deceased child, he or she was a part of the mother's soul that was taken from her.

Kourtney was armed with a complete medical history of her pregnancies and anything related. Her preparedness got me all the more excited about parenthood. I appreciated her willingness to share intimate details in our first meeting. Some of the details were a bit troublesome, though. I worried about her ability to carry a baby successfully once she revealed that she'd had a previous miscarriage.

"I have had a miscarriage," she said, "but it was when I was nineteen. So, it happened nearly six years ago. I was seventeen weeks along when I lost my daughter."

Her story was all too familiar. I wished I had worn earmuffs. I didn't want to hear things like that, but it gave us some common ground. At least she had an idea how I felt.

"I have had two pretty normal pregnancies with my two other kids," she said.

Okay. Things sound better.

"I had no problems with Lilly, but with Jace I had possible gestational diabetes and high blood pressure at the end. He was delivered a few weeks early."

I squirmed in my seat, and my eyes bugged out. I nodded and gave short, indifferent responses. I didn't want to reveal my disappointment. With the information she had given me, I doubted that surrogacy was going to work for her or me.

"After my pregnancy with Jace, I had really bad postpartum depression and anxiety. I am taking Prozac. I might be able to stop it if I carry your baby."

Hello! You will not take drugs with my baby in your body, crazy lady! This is turning into a nightmare.

"Did you take that during your past pregnancies?" I asked.

"No, I only needed it afterward."

Well, it was nice to know she *might* stop taking the medicine if she was pregnant with my baby. Ugh! There were too many red flags for her to be a surrogate for anyone. What doctor would let her carry a baby for someone else?

"We haven't really talked about the financial side of this," she said. "I want to have a baby for someone whether they pay me or not. If it's not you, it will be for someone else."

"We would certainly compensate you appropriately if you did this for us." I understood surrogacy to be expensive, and all of the costs would have to be covered by Cedric and me. We had resources available to us, but I needed to research surrogacy more to know how to get started in the right direction.

"I don't have insurance, either," she said. "That may change your mind. My husband does, but the premium is so expensive for covering family members that I am not on his plan."

Paying everything out of pocket was something we hadn't considered. "I'll check into it," I said. "Perhaps our insurance or your husband's will cover the pregnancy, even though it wouldn't be your baby. We would just pay the premium and any out-of-pocket stuff. What insurance does he have?"

"High Choice."

I lit up. That was my insurance. I could get all of my questions answered with one call. Money was a lesser concern. I was more focused on her health history and the fact that she was on Prozac. I knew that a woman wanted to go into pregnancy with as few problems as possible. So far, she was a walking health hazard, with psychotic tendencies to boot. That was overstating it, but I didn't want any drama at all. I already had a gut full with my own pregnancies.

Regardless, my wanting to be a mother again eclipsed anything she told me that was negative. I would have to get on my knees and hope that God would help us avoid a potential disaster, because my motherly instincts refused to say *no.* My heart was already in deep, and we had just scratched the surface.

"I'm not overly concerned about a miscarriage you had years ago. You've had two healthy babies since. If you were to get pregnant with my baby, you could probably get off the Prozac. You might not need it. I am not sure it's safe during pregnancy."

I hadn't really considered much of anything about the surrogacy, other than someone wanted to help give us a baby. There were so many facets to take into account during one meeting with Kourtney. There was bound to be a ghastly amount more that needed to be learned. For example, how exactly would one woman have a baby and then another take it from the hospital and claim it as her own? It wasn't an adoption. The baby was going to be genetically related to us and only us. Were we to fill out the birth certificate with our names on it and take home a baby—no questions asked?

"I'm thinking this has to be more complicated than we realize," I said. "Do you know anything about what happens after the baby is born? Like, whose name goes on the birth certificate?"

"I don't know," she responded. "We probably need to talk to an attorney. Maybe they would know about surrogacy."

"I'll do some research online and see how far I can get," I said.

"That's probably a good idea."

We parted ways. Each of us had a lot to think about and a lot to learn. Cedric and I had to figure out the business and legal end. She had the easy part: carrying the baby. I'd hoped that God would make things really simple, but it did not lean in that direction.

twelve

Information Overload

My new best friend was the Internet. There was so much to learn that I didn't know where to begin. I started with a simple search of *surrogacy* and found two types: traditional and gestational. *Traditional* meant that the carrier (surrogate) of the baby had a biological connection to it. In other words, her egg was used. Typically, the sperm of the intended father was used to fertilize said egg; therefore, the intended parents would have a partial genetic relationship to the baby. In *gestational* surrogacy, the carrier had no biological connection to the baby. Her uterus was borrowed to incubate another woman's fertilized egg. Because neither Cedric nor I had issues with our sperm and eggs, respectively, we would be able to use our own to make a baby that was biologically ours.

Surrogacy cost a lot. We would have to pay for everything pregnancy-related and then some. We had to cover expenses such as travel to appointments, maternity clothes, food, insurance, medical procedures, and postpartum care. The total cost varied from $45,000 to $120,000. We had socked away an amount somewhere in the middle of that range. It would be enough for a first-time surrogate's average compensation—that is, *if* insurance covered the pregnancy. Otherwise, we were sunk. Paying out of pocket would be too much.

I needed to know whether Kourtney would be covered under her husband's insurance, even if she was pregnant with someone else's baby. I called the insurance company with the intention of misleading the representative, because I was concerned that he or she would balk if I mentioned it was a surrogate pregnancy. I was paranoid that the company would flag my name or Kourtney's husband's and not pay medical expenses related to the surrogacy.

The palms of my hands perspired from nervousness. My mouth felt dry, like it was coated with cotton, when I asked to remain anonymous and then lied, telling them my husband was a member of the insurance group. Lies and deception weren't in my repertoire.

The first three people I spoke with didn't know what *surrogacy* meant. When I told them another woman was going to carry my baby, which was made from my husband's sperm and my egg, it blew their minds. Their initial responses were simply, "No, we don't do that."

"Let me talk to someone who might know what I'm talking about," I said.

"I'll let you speak with my supervisor."

Even after I talked to the head of the department, the answer was the same, "No, we don't cover surrogacy."

So I had to take a slightly different, tackier approach with him. "If I secretly get pregnant by someone other than my husband, but I am on his insurance, you are saying you will not cover my pregnancy?"

There was silence. I knew they were obligated to cover pregnancy, but the word *surrogacy* was throwing everyone for a loop. I crossed my fingers, hoping for an affirmative answer.

"Uh, let me call legal."

"You do that and get back to me."

It wasn't long before I received a call. "We do cover surrogacy," the supervisor said.

"Are you sure?" I asked. I was about to explode with excitement.

"Yes, as long as the pregnant person was a member or a dependent and on whoever's policy before the pregnancy."

Just to make sure, I asked again, "You are certain a woman can carry someone else's embryo in her body and still be covered by insurance as long as she was on a policy beforehand?"

"Yes," he said. "We don't care how the baby got there. If she is a member or a dependent, she is covered. The pregnancy is covered, and the baby is covered."

"Thank you. You just made my day."

"Sorry for the trouble," he said. "This is a first for me."

I laughed. "Now you know."

Hallelujah! It was an incredibly huge step forward. The insurance Kourtney and Nathan had was very good and covered a large percentage of the expenses. I immediately informed Kourtney of this but told her that she would have to sign up in October of the current year to be on the policy in 2011. We would make the premium payments for her portion starting in January. It bought us a few months to make sure we knew exactly what was going on. However, I did worry it would give her time to come to her senses and back out of the surrogacy. The thought was fleeting, though, because I had too much else to do.

I continued my research and stumbled across information that was not encouraging. While searching *surrogacy in Oklahoma*, I learned that it was not recognized as a legal process; there were no laws governing it. In other words, old-fashioned Oklahoma wasn't really up to speed on how a surrogate helped infertile couples have a child who was genetically related to them. In Oklahoma's thinking, a baby in a woman's womb belonged to her, despite the genetics. Apparently, lawmakers believed that anyone who compensated someone else to have her baby or received compensation for having a baby was a child trafficker. Just like the insurance people, they didn't want to learn about surrogacy, because it was a relatively new concept in Oklahoma. It required research for them to fully understand that surrogacy was just an alternative approach to building families, and, obviously, no one was willing to invest the time. The easiest thing was to say no.

We desperately needed a lawyer. I felt frustrated at the legal mess it was turning into. I hoped that an expert would clarify it for us. I spent more time on the computer looking for a surrogacy attorney. Of course, there were zero in Oklahoma. I finally came across an adoption attorney who claimed to have experience with surrogacy cases. It was better than nothing. She worked for an uppity firm that catered to some big-name clients, so I figured she was trustworthy enough. I called on August 9 to set up an appointment with her. I had to leave a message with the secretary, and I spent a few nervous hours before she called back.

"Janice would like to meet you. How about tomorrow at 9:00 a.m.?"

I had no clue what was on our family's schedule, but I wanted to get the ball rolling as quickly as possible. Without hesitation, I said, "Absolutely! We'll be there."

The very next day, we dressed in our Sunday best and drove almost three hours to meet the only attorney in the state advertising that she knew something about surrogacy. We parked our dirty little car, caked with bugs and red dirt, in front of the tallest building in the city. Window washers dangled precariously from its façade, squeegeeing liquid off the glass and giving the skyscraper a pristine appearance. We walked onto an elevator that had more buttons than all of the clothes in my walk-in closet.

After going up twenty or so floors, we entered the menacing doors of the law firm. Every fixture, pen, and person was poised and polished. Neither of us had any experience with lawyers, so it was intimidating. We were greeted by a friendly receptionist who paged the attorney.

Janice quickly appeared and introduced herself. She was well spoken and nice and seemed eager to get started. She didn't allow much time for small talk and got right to the reason we were there.

"Why are you considering surrogacy?" Janice asked.

I cringed. I hated to explain our recent history to anyone, especially about Samuel, because it was still fresh.

"We have had really bad luck with our pregnancies," I said. "Two of the last three were miscarriages in the second trimester, and the third one was very complicated. We had a premature baby boy born almost three months too early. As a result, he died hours later."

She responded, "As you know, I am an adoption attorney. I have represented very few surrogacies, and those were out of state. I have never done one in Oklahoma."

That was not good to hear. My assumption that a high-powered, reputable law firm would have the most knowledgeable, seasoned attorneys was quashed.

"There is a lot of legal paperwork with a surrogacy . . . in other states," she said. "Because Oklahoma has no laws governing surrogacy, no amount of paperwork will guarantee that you go home with a baby, even if it is biologically yours."

The more she talked, the more depressed I felt. "Kenzie, you will not be the legal mother of any baby born to a surrogate, even if it was your egg. Cedric, you could be recognized as the father as long as the surrogate's husband signed a Denial of Paternity document, and you signed an Acceptance of Paternity document. That would legally put your name on the birth certificate. Kenzie, your name will never be on there. In fact, you will have to legally adopt the child. You will have to go through the same process as any adopting couple: home studies, background checks, and possibly fostering a child before adopting yours."

What she said was like a kick in the head. There was no logic to it. I would be subject to home studies and background checks? I felt as if I were a pedophile who would have to be watched around children. I couldn't believe that I, with scarcely a speeding ticket on my record, was being treated like a criminal. This was my flesh and blood I would be taking home. I already had a daughter whom I treasured, and I had lain in a hospital bed in an attempt to save Samuel. My reward for being a caring, loving mother was to be subject to evaluations, inspections, and a court's approval before I could take possession of my baby.

"Seriously? I have to adopt a child who is genetically mine to begin with?"

"Yes. There is no way around it. When the baby is here, everyone involved will have to go to court. The surrogate will be required to relinquish maternal rights. She could easily refuse and keep the baby. You have no rights to the baby in the eyes of the courts in the state of Oklahoma."

I sat stone-faced. It seemed as if all of the air had been sucked out of the room. I didn't know whether it would be possible to get my own baby. If I did, how could I explain it later? Would anyone believe I was his or her real biological mother? Would the child be harassed his entire life, because he was a surrogate baby? Would he be confused and hate me? I had already been deprived of the ability to carry the child in my own womb. I wasn't going to be on the birth certificate, either.

She proceeded, "I need to ask just a few more questions that may or may not make things easier for you."

Easier? Really? I thought.

"Does the potential surrogate or her husband have Native American ancestors?"

"I don't think so. At least I haven't ever heard them mention anything like that. I'll need to ask them to make sure. Why?"

"If either of them does, the tribe they are associated with would get first dibs on any children they gave up for adoption, due to the Indian Child Welfare Act. That would include your child she carried."

I thought I had heard it all, but that was by far the most absurd thing she had said. In addition to being treated like criminals, we now owed our child to a certain race of individuals who had been wronged a couple hundred years ago, albeit by very cruel people. Yet I shared none of the prejudices of these long-ago settlers, nor, to my knowledge, were any of my ancestors even in America at that time. A tribe with zero vested interest could swoop in, take our baby who was 100 percent genetically related to us, and claim it as their own, solely based on the ethnicity of a surrogate or her husband. *Kudos, Oklahoma. Kudos.* While I ruminated on that bit of information, she asked whether we had a contract.

"A what?" I asked. Even though I had heard her, I was completely surprised, not having a clue what she referred to.

"A contract," she repeated. "It sort of lays out what the expectations are in the surrogacy. For example, what if she has to go on bed rest? Who will pay for her children's day care, because she is no longer able to care for them?"

"We assumed we would."

"I would expect you to do that, but there is a legal snag you need to be aware of. You can reimburse her only for reasonable maternity expenses. You can't give her any extras, because Oklahoma law considers that child trafficking."

"That is the only thing you have told us today that does not surprise me! I had read something like that online." It was ironic, because Oklahoma had no laws about surrogacy.

As I suspected, the legal side of surrogacy would be the most difficult part. I was disheartened. It would seemingly be impossible to get the deal done. It was like butterflies trying to thrive in the cold winters of Oklahoma.

"There's another thing to consider," she said. "Although a contract is a great guideline between you and the surrogate, it is not a legal document. No court will uphold it. If she drank alcohol, and the contract stated that she couldn't, it doesn't matter."

On that pleasant note, our hour was up. Because Janice seemed to know the process, we chose to play it safe and retain her. The $195 an hour would be costly but doable. It would be easier to fight any court battles with an attorney who knew the legalese.

The consultation took the wind out of our sails. I understood that the laws were in place to protect children, but Cedric and I were not adopting another family's child. There was no paternity or guardianship battle or a question about tribal roots. This was our baby whom we already loved and our hearts ached for. No one had an interest in the child more than us. It insulted us to be scrutinized like people whose problems had provoked the creation of the rules.

Still, a flicker of hope burned bright enough for us to want to endure the trials to come. Another baby to hold was more important than signing court documents, having my name on a birth certificate, or transferring ownership of a baby to its loving and responsible biological parents. We had plenty to stew about, but getting angry about something we couldn't change wouldn't help anything. It seemed as if we were just going to have to play the legal game.

I gave Kourtney an earful during our return trip. We planned a lunch the following Sunday so that our families could meet, and we could talk specifics. Meanwhile, I intended to research the topics our attorney had discussed with us, especially the contract. We needed to let Kourtney know our expectations of her sooner, rather than later. We wanted to give her time to soak it in—but not really. I just wanted her to have my baby. Time and information gave her a chance to change her mind. I wanted to expedite the process as much as I could.

Surrogacy contracts were not easy to find online. I discovered that people pretty much had to create the document on their own. Luckily, one woman was willing to post her template online, so that was what I used. It was about ten pages long in eight-point font. It was overkill; however, it covered a lot of topics that I had not even thought about. For instance, "How many babies would the surrogate be willing to carry to term if multiple embryos were implanted?" There was something called *selective reduction*. The surrogate and the intended parents could agree to abort one or more of the embryos if they didn't want more than a certain number. Aborting embryos was not an option for us, so that was something we would all need to agree on beforehand.

The contract contained mountains of stipulations; most of them protected the intended parents. A few examples were, "If the surrogate smokes during pregnancy, she forfeits all compensation. If the surrogate miscarries, she only receives payment up to the month of miscarriage." There was an itemized list of each dollar that would be given to the surrogate, for what purpose, and in which month of pregnancy.

The details of the contract were staggering, but each one could be altered to my liking. In reality, it didn't matter what it said before or after I tweaked it, because the state of Oklahoma wasn't going to honor any of it in a court of law. It was merely for the peace of mind of the parties involved. Regardless, I modified it exactly as I wanted to, and I planned to present it to Kourtney during our lunch meeting.

thirteen

New Beginnings

I waited with eager anticipation for the day our families would finally get to meet. Much like a fiancé meeting the future in-laws for the first time, interacting with Kourtney's family made the surrogacy seem more official.

Sunday finally came. After church, we drove twenty minutes to a nearby town for lunch. Kourtney, along with her husband, Nathan, and their two kids, Lilly and Jace, welcomed us into their home and essentially into their lives. Their house was cute and decorated with the latest trends I often saw and admired in magazines, but I was more enamored with her children's artwork, which adorned one particular wall. When gazed upon, each one was certain to evoke a special memory for her. Those were the decorations I missed—the smeared handprints, half-colored masterpieces ripped from coloring books, and original, hand-drawn versions of "Mommy" and "Daddy." I listened to the joyful noises her children made as they played together. Those sounds—*any* cry, squeal, laugh, or even moan—were a God-given privilege and a direct reflection of what being a mom was all about for me. My heart ached for that. I wanted another chance to be called "Mommy" again.

Our families had to be comfortable with each other, considering the intimacy of surrogacy. Private moments between an expecting couple were going to be shared between two couples. Ultrasounds, appointments, and the delivery were only a few of the experiences that would evoke all sorts of emotions in each of us. Preparing for that reality was important, and the contract was the first step. We really needed to be on the same frequency for the process to work.

I opened with what I thought was the most crucial part: all issues related to abortion determined how much further our relationship went. Because I had no legal say in any part of the surrogacy, I had to be sure she wouldn't terminate the baby. The only out she had was if her life was in grave danger because of the pregnancy. All of my doctors were against abortion but would end a pregnancy before allowing the mother to die. I believed that portion of the contract to be one of the most challenging issues. She had a family she needed to care for. Why should she have to sacrifice herself for a baby who wasn't hers? I hadn't given her the contract yet. I wanted her responses to my questions to be as unbiased as possible.

"How do you feel about abortion?" I asked. "I mean . . . at what point would you want doctors to intervene and end the pregnancy if there was a problem?"

"I don't believe in aborting babies," she said. "Life begins at conception, in my opinion. I would never terminate. I would do everything in my power to save the baby, until my life was in imminent danger. I hope we don't have to go there."

"I agree," I said. "The doctors I know won't let it go that far. Otherwise, they would possibly lose two patients. It's a hard thing to consider, but it is reality."

The topic was unappealing, and I never wanted to revisit it. However, I got the answer I had hoped for, so I was happy.

I rehashed our meeting with the attorney, because Kourtney and Nathan would play critical roles in the legal process. I admired her passionate responses as I explained the ignorant Oklahoma laws. I trusted that she was on my side and would fight for me, if it came to that.

"I don't want to keep a baby who is not mine. Why would I? I am volunteering to do this for someone else. If I wanted more kids, I would have my own. It is ridiculous that they will make you guys jump through a million hoops just to adopt your own babies, but they will give a child back to its drug-addicted, abusive parents, simply because they went to a few weeks of rehab."

I responded with my own spirited monologue. "I know! It makes no sense. You would think a genetic test would end it. Nope. It's completely asinine! One specific thing the attorney asked was whether you or Nathan had any Native American heritage. If you do, it is an issue because there is a law that gives tribes the right to adopt a baby with Native American ancestry before anyone else can."

She rolled her eyes. "I don't think either of us does. It has never been documented anyway."

"Whew! That's one thing in our favor."

"That's a stupid law," she said.

"I agree. I brought the contract for you to look at in the near future. It's very detailed and overwhelming at first glance, but it spells everything out and gives dollar amounts that we think would be fair for pregnancy-related expenses. Just to be clear, the contract isn't really a legally binding document, even if we all sign it. We'll need to have a lot of faith and trust in one another . . . trust that we will follow through with the terms."

She almost seemed offended. "I am not doing this for the money. I want to help you guys have a baby. You don't have to pay me anything, and I would still do it. We'll look it over later. I don't have time today; I'm going to a party."

I was glad the subject had changed. The last thing I wanted to do was insult her. I didn't think I had, because she asked, "Would you like to go to a makeup-and-jewelry party with me?"

"Sure! It sounds like fun!"

"Great! You'll get to meet a ton of my friends and family," she said.

I wanted to say no once she said that. I was not into mingling, especially with people I didn't know. However, I was pretty sure "No" would soon drop from my vocabulary. I wasn't going to refuse anything she asked of me, because she had agreed to carry my baby. I would have eaten road kill for her. I hated wearing makeup and jewelry, but I sensed that a tube of lipstick and a bracelet were the cheapest items I was going to buy in the relationship.

On the way to the party, we had some time to discuss the surrogacy.

"My parents are not real thrilled about me being a surrogate," she said. "They think it's too risky for my health and emotionally draining to give up a baby."

I had a lot of respect for my parents, and, generally, I was likely to do whatever they advised me to do. I didn't like to hear that her parents were opposed to her decision. I figured they might be able to sway her opinion on the matter. I did what I could to keep her focused. "It's not like the baby is related to them. And you have all the kids you want. I don't see the big deal. People just don't understand the importance of surrogacy unless they have had fertility problems."

"Don't worry," she said with a sly grin. "I've never done what my parents have told me to do. In fact, the more they oppose, the more I push back."

I was sure I had more than her parents to contend with. Who knew how many of her friends thought surrogacy was a bad idea?

"If you don't want to do this, please tell me now," I said. I winced a little, because I was afraid of getting an answer I didn't want to hear.

"I am going to do this," she said.

I'll bet her parents had fits with her growing up, I thought. Stubbornness and independence were okay with me. It showed that she was ambitious and driven to accomplish her goals, which gave me confidence that she would be our surrogate.

At the party, I was way out of my comfort zone. I was surrounded by Kourtney's family and friends, all of whom knew one another. All eyes were fixed on us—mainly on me. I knew that women sized one another up as they walked through a door. I was guilty of doing the same, especially if it was a *new girl*. With that much estrogen running rampant in one room, it was not difficult to guess who they whispered about. I was on display. If I could peer into their minds, I'm sure I would have heard things like, "Why can't she have her own kids?" or "How much is she paying Kourtney to have her baby?" or "How did she convince Kourtney to sacrifice her body for a stranger?" I was either a really good people reader or really paranoid; maybe it was a little of both. Considering that I had breasts and a vagina, too, I put my money on the former.

Because I was the new girl, I had to be on my best behavior. First impressions were important. Typically, I was witty with a touch of sarcasm in most situations. The usual term of endearment I received was "smartass." Yet because I didn't want the ladies at the party to be offended, I chose to don a shyer, more reserved mask. I believed it would be safer.

Kourtney paraded me around from one person to the next. Last but not least, I was introduced to her mother. As I had anticipated, it was awkward. Her mother's eyes were so big and bright blue, they scared me a little. I wasn't sure whether they were normally that big or if she was surprised to see me. Seriously, they were huge.

"Mom, this is Kenzie, the girl whose baby I will be carrying," Kourtney said, giggling at the phrasing of her words.

"Oh, hi!" said her mother, as she walked away.

Yep. That summed it up.

"I think that went well," I said.

Kourtney shook her head. I suppose I should have shrugged it off as well. It bugged me, though, when people didn't approve of me or the things I was doing. Maybe I shouldn't have cared, but I didn't have it in me to intentionally drive a wedge between Kourtney and her parents. Although, when it came down to it, I was going to do what I believed God wanted me to do. There probably were people who were going to be offended. I wasn't forcing Kourtney into anything. In fact, the surrogacy was her idea. My husband and I happened to be in the right place at the right time and knew the right person: Diane. God was the biggest protagonist in the circumstances that had brought us to the present. He had a knack for getting things done exactly the right way.

After my encounter with Kourtney's mother, the last thing I wanted was to be showered with more attention. With vanity mirrors propped up in front of us, Kourtney and I sat in a corner of the room, applying makeup like drunk clowns while decked out in gaudy jewelry that completed the ensemble. We had some good laughs; it was a definite ice breaker for us. Our relationship started to feel more like a friendship.

Samuel's memorial service was a few weeks away, and I couldn't have thought of a better, more personal event to invite my new friend to than that, especially since I was giving the sermon.

"Would you want to come to church with us September 5? I am giving the sermon. It's more of a tribute to honor Samuel's memory."

"We wouldn't miss it!" Kourtney said.

"I'm kind of excited to do it that day, because it was his due date."

"That's awesome! Don't you think it's going to be hard? I mean . . . aren't you afraid you'll break down?"

"No. I'm prepared. I wrote a bunch of stuff down the morning Samuel died. It was weird. Words just started coming to me. I believed my writing was inspired by God, so I am going with that. I couldn't have thought of it on my own. It was coming in way too fast, and I am not that creative. I was an emotional mess at the time and not thinking clearly. It's going to be good, because God wrote it. I will just be his messenger."

I was filled with delight. I knew it would be Samuel's finest hour, and I got the privilege of being his voice.

❧❦

I put the surrogacy on the back burner for a short while to focus my time and attention on Samuel's memorial sermon. It needed to be polished, and I wanted to ensure that the pacing would fill up the allotted time. The pastor had put it on my shoulders weeks ago to deliver the message to the congregation, and he was emphatic about having it be the precise length of time. Apparently, members of the older generation didn't like their routines messed with. That was his excuse anyway. It always seemed as if *he* was the one rushing home to watch the Sunday football games. Either way, I took it upon myself to call him a few days before the service, and I had a little fun at his expense.

"Hey, Pastor James. I've been practicing my sermon. It should take up about five minutes, so you'll have plenty of time to give your message."

"What? Are you serious? Tell me you're kidding?"

"No, I'm not. Is that a problem?"

There was silence on the other end for an uncomfortable amount of time.

"You have a sermon ready, right?" I asked.

"No!"

I couldn't contain myself any longer. Because he was obviously mad, I thought I'd better tell the truth before he cussed at me.

I burst out laughing. "Okay, okay, I'm kidding!"

"Don't do that! It's not funny. You about gave me a heart attack. Seriously, though . . . it's longer than that . . . right?"

I snickered. "Yes. I'm good to go."

fourteen

His Message

The fifth arrived more quickly than I liked. We went to church early that morning, thinking it would calm my nerves. I stood at the pulpit with my sermon in hand, staring out at the empty pews. *It's not so bad up here. I got this.*

We usually occupied the cheap seats in the sanctuary; however, I chose to sit alone in the front pew. I didn't want to get emotional before the service even started, seeing my relatives and friends who were there to support me. I had extra family members attending, as well as Kourtney's family and Diane and her husband.

The pastor went through his routine of meet and greet, singing, offering, and scripture. Then it was my turn to take the stage. I could feel everyone's eyes boring into me. I was so nervous; my mouth was dry and sticky. I was sweating so much; I was afraid it would show through my gray shirt. And to top it all off, I got the sudden urge to use the bathroom. I had stupidly worn a pair of heavy sandals that made lots of noise with every step. Before climbing the stairs to the pulpit, I kicked my sandals off under the pew and walked up to the stage barefoot. For some reason, that action made me feel more like one of Jesus's twelve disciples. I was extremely humbled by the opportunity to speak in front of people about one of God's servants, my Samuel.

I stood next to the pastor as he prayed over my sermon. Then I was left alone to deliver a message about our little baby boy, who, despite living a few short hours, had a great impact on many lives.

O Lord Almighty, if you will only look upon your servant's misery and remember me, and not forget your servant but give her a son, then I will give him to the Lord for all the days of his life.—1 Samuel 1:11

Hannah, Samuel's mother, prayed this prayer; she had been barren and yearned for a son. Yet she was giving up what she was asking for. She promised God her son and she gave him up soon after he was born and he became one of God's wisest prophets. Sometimes the Bible is so surreal that it is hard to believe.

I attempted from the beginning of my pregnancy to model myself after Hannah. I fell short, in that I promised God my son; however, I was thinking I would raise him to serve God here on earth and not have to give him up so quickly. My Samuel didn't live long, but he was able to serve God, and he did it perfectly.

How can an unborn child serve God? Through prayer, sacrifice, and love, Samuel brought each and every one of us to our knees, petitioning to the Creator of the heavens and the earth and everything in it.

Far be it from me that I should sin against the Lord by failing to pray for you.—1 Samuel 12:23

I know how hard many of us prayed for a healthy pregnancy and baby. We asked God for a miracle. Prayers went up more frequently and more earnestly. Prayers came from all over the United States, from strangers I had never met, and even from individuals who don't normally pray. All of these prayers came before God's child had ever entered the world. You committed yourselves to the Lord through prayer and petitioning on Samuel's behalf. You were serving your Lord by doing what he commanded. If I had never been pregnant with Samuel, that means each of you would have had fewer conversations with God.

Greater love has no one than this that he lay down his life for his friends.—John 15:13

I discovered it is humanly possible to love something more than myself. So much more that I sacrificed my comfort, time, body, and spirit. All of it was without any guarantees. Too many times, I heard ugly words and phrases like "terminate," "fatal maternal infection," "major bleeding," "deformities," and "low chance of baby's survival." It was too many frightening things to hear at weekly appointments.

Samuel gave me a chance to sacrifice myself for him and put aside my comforts to experience his God-breathed life. I knew it might be for a short while, if at all. I endured many struggles and faced disheartening realities, but I pressed on, knowing this was only a small piece of a giant puzzle.

God gave us his son and sacrificed him for all of humanity. Without my experience with Samuel, I would still be taking God's sacrifice for granted.

Be devoted to one another in brotherly love. Honor one another above yourselves. Be joyful in hope, patient in affliction, faithful in prayer.—Romans 12:10, 12

In times of tragedy, you are faced with two options. You can be consumed with fear and self-destruct, or you can grab onto everything you love and hang on tight, enduring the bumps on God's chosen path. The love we shared for Samuel and the love God has for us led us to the latter. We have formed bonds with family and friends that no hardship will overcome. We have been taught to share that love with others, in spite of our troubles. Samuel gave us a fresh start. Many times, marriages fall apart during stressful events. Our marriage was strengthened, and we learned to lean on one another. He showed us how important we are to each other. Samuel helped us bring the meaning of faith and family back into focus. Though we can't hug on him now, we can share in his triumph over death and hug on each other until we see him again.

Samuel was a true gift from God. We are forever changed, because of him. Good did come from our harrowing situation. When you are faced with troubles, please remember this message. I can't guarantee your lives will be without heartache and uncertainty. This world *will* fail you, but I can guarantee that God won't fail you.

To my dearest Samuel,

I hope someday these verses apply to me, just as they have to you: I have fought the good fight, I have finished the race, I have kept the faith. Now there is in store for me the crown of righteousness, which the Lord, the righteous Judge, will award me on that day—and not only to me, but also to all who have longed for his appearing.—2 Timothy 4:7–8

I never shed a tear. My voice never wavered. I stood strong and determined to share with the people that even the smallest, most fragile human has a purpose. I was privileged that God had chosen me to be Samuel's mother, and I was honored that he chose me to give his message conveyed through the life of a baby boy I had called my own for a brief moment in time.

fifteen

IVF 101

In mid-September, I had my first appointment with the fertility doctor to discuss surrogacy. The doctor was no stranger to me, because I had visited him prior to my pregnancy with Samuel. I had looked up his profile on his clinic's website, and it said he had experience with surrogate invitro fertilization (IVF). In fact, he was the only doctor in Oklahoma who would do IVF for a gestational surrogacy. He was my only hope. The consultation was mainly for informational purposes. I was there so he could determine whether I was even a candidate for IVF.

"I am not a Hollywood doctor who does surrogate IVFs, because a woman doesn't want to get fat. I do surrogate cases only if there is a real need. Because you have lost three babies for unknown reasons and because you have been through the gauntlet with medical testing, I think you are a good candidate for surrogacy. I do IVF procedures all the time and have a very high success rate with women carrying the baby to term. Surrogacy is no different. The only extra step is to get both you and your surrogate's hormone levels adjusted just right so that the embryo transfer goes as smooth and quickly as possible."

"I'm not that familiar with IVF. I know eggs get fertilized in a test tube or something, but what exactly goes on?" I asked.

"First, I will make sure both you and the surrogate are healthy by performing ultrasounds and blood work. I'll look for any structural abnormalities during the ultrasound. The blood work is to check your hormone levels, the presence of blood-borne diseases, and general blood chemistry. Once I determine you are healthy and I have figured out your biological clocks, you'll inject yourself with hormones that stimulate egg production and development. At the same time, your surrogate will inject herself with hormones to prepare her uterus to be the most hospitable for your fertilized eggs. Your husband will be required to provide a semen sample sometime before that, so it can be mixed with your eggs."

I tried to keep a straight face, but I giggled like a seventh-grader learning about the human reproductive system.

"You mean, he has to . . . um . . . in a cup. . . . Where exactly will he do that?"

He cracked a smile. "We have a room here. Once he makes his deposit, we will examine the specimen to ensure that it is clean and viable."

It better be clean, I thought.

"At a later date, your surrogate will go through a mock embryo transfer to determine where I need to implant the embryos in her uterus. One of the negatives of IVF is all of the blood work and ultrasounds we will need from you. We have to monitor those levels daily. It is very important for us to monitor the hormone levels and egg maturation."

"Uh, I live two and half hours away," I said.

"You'll need to drive every day or find someplace to stay nearby. Once the eggs are mature, you will inject yourself with a medicine that causes the eggs to release from the ovaries. After that, I'll go in via ultrasound and use a catheter to retrieve them. They will be fertilized with your husband's sperm. The embryologist will let them grow and determine the embryos' viability. Some will thrive, and some will perish. At that point, your part is over and your surrogate's part is just beginning. Depending on your agreement with your surrogate, I'll implant a certain number of thriving ones, and any others will be stored or discarded."

"We'll be storing any extras," I said. "We're not throwing away our babies."

"We'll do whatever you want," he said. "Once the embryos are implanted, your surrogate will continue to inject herself with hormones that will help the embryos stick to the lining in her uterus. She will have to do the injections for several months. If the first attempt doesn't work, we can try again with the extra embryos."

I shook my head. Too much information had been thrown at me. I didn't want to have to think about a second attempt. I had barely understood what would happen in the first attempt. "This is all overwhelming. How do you time all of this so perfectly?"

"Pretty amazing, isn't it? Don't worry," he said, "it's my job, and I have been doing it for a while. I've gotten pretty good at it. When you start your next menstrual cycle, you need to call me. That is when the process begins."

That sounded thrilling to me. After much reflection on the consultation with the doctor, I was fairly certain he was the only man who could be excited about my period and my hormone fluctuations. My own husband could barely muster up the courage to buy a box of pads at the store, let alone be enthusiastic about my monthly visitor and the many personalities that accompanied it.

I was anxious to call Kourtney and tell her about everything I had learned at the consultation. I didn't get very deep into the conversation before she brought up my past pregnancy problems.

"I had a friend ask me if maybe the cause of your problems was because of your embryos being bad or something. Do you think that was the problem? I'm not sure I would want to deal with that."

I choked back my tears. I was not only completely offended, but it saddened me to have her doubt what I had told her about my pregnancy history. I already considered myself inadequate because I couldn't carry my own children. My babies were being insulted as well. I got the sick feeling that she didn't want to move forward with the surrogacy.

I tried to reassure her. "It's not the embryos. The doctors tested the babies and the placenta after I had given birth. There were never any issues whatsoever. Something was wrong with me that they could never figure out."

Reliving the nightmare was too much. I couldn't hold back my emotions. I quickly said I needed to go. I burst into tears, thinking it was all over before it even began. It had just been an illusion.

I stopped at a sporting goods store, still in tears, to do some therapy shopping. I roamed the aisles for a while before I composed myself and sent Kourtney a text: IF YOU DON'T WANT TO DO THIS, TELL ME NOW. I DON'T WANT TO PRESSURE YOU INTO ANYTHING.

I had said that to her a thousand times, and each time it made my heart ache. I wanted a baby so bad. I hated even to plant that seed in her head, but I would rather have known then than the day after the eggs were fertilized.

She texted me: I'M NOT BACKING OUT. I'M READY TO DO THIS. I'LL ALWAYS BE HONEST AND UP FRONT WITH YOU GUYS.

I started bawling again. My brain told me I was satisfied with our little family—just the three of us—but my soul screamed something different. The little flash of hope that I regained after Diane first told us about Kourtney was always shadowed by despair I thought I had overcome. Each day was one step closer; however, each time I sensed uncertainty from Kourtney about whether the surrogacy would come to realization, it sent me back in time and rekindled the terrible grief and emptiness I had felt just after Samuel passed. I thought he was my last chance at motherhood. I lamented all over again and was angry at God for allowing the surrogacy idea to be planted in my brain. Depending on someone else to provide me with a miracle baby reinforced how little control I had. It was painfully obvious that involvement in a surrogacy would test my endurance for cultivating hope.

A few weeks after the consultation, I started my menstrual cycle. I made a very early morning, two-and-a-half-hour drive to the clinic to get blood work and an ultrasound done.

"I'm surprised you work on the weekends," I said, using small talk to distract myself while being probed internally with the ultrasound tool.

The doctor chuckled. "Mother Nature doesn't work around our convenience. Everything looks good. I'll be checking back with you. I anticipate seeing Kourtney next week sometime."

I was happy to be making forward progress. Nothing was going real fast, and I expected it to remain that way. It was barely October. We still had to wait until January 2011 for her insurance to kick in before we could go much further. As planned, Kourtney had her appointment almost a week after mine.

She called me as soon as she got out. "All went well. I like the doctor. He said everything was good. I have a benign ovarian cyst that will need to be removed. He doesn't want anything interfering. It will be an extra expense, but I will be on Nathan's insurance, and they will cover most of it."

"Sounds good to me," I said, trying to conceal my enthusiasm. "So, we wait for January and then get busy."

☙❧

Cedric completed the only other surrogacy-related task that could be done before the New Year. He made his one physical contribution to the process: sperm. That was an important part, but he got off pretty easy, compared to what was in store for Kourtney and me.

The remainder of 2010, thankfully, was uneventful. We spent our first Thanksgiving, Christmas, and New Year's in our new house, which seemed empty with only the three of us celebrating. We devoted time to reflect on the events of the last year. A lot had taken place: a pregnancy, the loss of a child, the closing of one womb, and the opening of another. Each event shaped us into new people, but we still had the same old vision: we wanted a baby to occupy space, not only in our home, but also in our hearts.

sixteen

Surrogacy Pains

The year 2011 came in with a bang . . . to our wallets. We made the first of Kourtney's insurance premium payments to the tune of about $600. It was small change, compared to the remaining balance that we would owe in the future. Once she got pregnant, we would be giving her monthly compensation to cover extra expenses that she or her family might incur. We were fortunate to live off Cedric's paycheck, so I had been able to save my teaching salary from the previous five years. We would spend those savings on the surrogacy. It was approximately the national average cost for a first-time, private surrogacy; therefore, we had put that amount in the contract. The money would cover everything, except for unforeseen circumstances, such as emergency surgery or long-term postpartum care. We hoped that Kourtney would agree with those figures.

We met up with Kourtney at her home again in early February. She had a surprise for us but wouldn't say what it was over the phone. So we drove to her house and were greeted by her family—and a litter of puppies.

With a devious smile and the signed contract in hand, she asked, "You guys want a puppy for your new baby, don't you?"

Cedric and I glanced at each other, exchanging grimaces. We already had one dog and eleven cats, but she had us cornered. What were we supposed to do? Say no to the woman who had volunteered to carry our baby for nine months? We had no choice but to take a puppy home with us. All I could think of was chasing two dogs through the countryside with a baby on my hip and leashes in my hand. We had not had good experiences with owning two dogs at once. Our previous dogs had loved to run far, far away.

"Uh, sure. Why not? Who doesn't love a new puppy?" *What the hell am I saying?*

A few weeks post–puppy adoption, the fertility doctor called and arranged a meeting with a psychologist for both of our families to attend. It was a requirement of the fertility clinic to make sure both couples in the surrogacy agreed about the process, its complexities, and the possible outcomes. It didn't sound too bad; it was probably a good idea for a third party to analyze each of us, just in case anyone was holding something back. I assumed that we had formed a trustworthy alliance. Yet I worried just a little, because I never knew what kind of voodoo curses shrinks put on people to get them to expose their darkest secrets. I hoped Kourtney wasn't going to reveal that she had multiple personalities or had some strange fetish that would raise red flags to the psychologist.

At our appointment, I could tell we were all in for a big treat. The four of us waited in a small private room that contained shelves crammed with books and brochures on sex, sexual fantasies, how-tos on pleasing your mate, and much more. We covered our mouths to muffle our giggles and tee-hees.

"Hey," I whispered, "are we going to have to look at those?"

"Oh, Lord," said Kourtney. "She must be a sex therapist!"

Cedric was concerned. "We're at the correct address, right?"

"I don't need help," Nathan said. "I know what to do."

We couldn't contain ourselves. Four adults trapped in a room with sex books provided for some comedic relief.

"I dare you to look at one," I said to Cedric.

"No, she might walk in and think I'm a pervert."

"Is she going to talk to us about sex?" Kourtney asked. "We have kids, it's not like we don't know how to do it."

"Well, I am not talking," Cedric said.

"What if she has props?" I joked.

"We aren't even here for that," said Nathan. "I'm leaving if we have to talk about sex."

After much discussion of what we were not willing to talk about, we were interrupted by a woman who appeared to be a throwback from the '60s. By the way she looked and talked, all I could think was, "She is going to smoke pot and talk about sex!"

"Hey, guys! I'm Wendy. I'm an infertility counselor. Your doctor asked me to meet with you and talk about your surrogacy. I usually help couples who have had some sort of trouble conceiving, but I also meet with couples considering adoption or surrogacy."

All of us let out a sigh of relief.

"We noticed the books on the shelves and were a little . . . uh . . . concerned," I said.

She laughed. "I know we are here to discuss surrogacy. I have spoken with your doctor. Don't worry. But we can talk about sex if you want to."

"No!" we said in unison.

After that one awkward introduction, two hours, three interviews, and $400 later, we all left without being escorted to the nearest mental hospital in restraints. Our alliance was still intact, we had not been forced to talk about sex, and we got the go-ahead to implant our embryo into Kourtney's body—nothing too out of the ordinary.

We experienced a lull in the surrogacy lasting about two months, waiting for the fertility doctor to time everything just right. The idle time let me imagine all sorts of nightmarish scenarios that might occur. I found it difficult to think positively, due to my history with bad pregnancies and dead babies. At some point, I would have to let the past be the past—if that was possible. My empty arms had a tendency to remind me every day.

In April, Kourtney had surgery to remove her ovarian cyst. It was not a major surgery, nor was it a danger to a baby, but the doctor wanted to start without any anomalies. The surgery was our responsibility. *Ka-ching.* I bit my lip as I wrote out the co-pay check for $1,000. Tight-fistedness was not an option, though. I just hoped it would all be worth it. I was not going to be happy with Kourtney if she changed her mind right after we handed our doctor the up-front, nonrefundable fee of $15,000 for the IVF. If the embryo were to be implanted in me, I would not have hesitated to spend that amount of money, but investing in someone else was different. I couldn't control Kourtney's feelings, thoughts, or, more specifically, the way she took care of her body and a baby living inside of her. It required more trust than I had in anyone.

God would not be my favorite entity, either, if we invested that much and lost another baby at five or six months of gestation. I knew I should trust him, but over the years I had discovered that this didn't mean things would go the way I wanted them to. That was the hardest part about being a Christian: dealing with insufferable calamities while knowing the one who loved me the most was allowing it to happen, just so he could bring a better ending that wasn't yet visible to me.

In late May the nurse from the clinic called to inform me that I would start egg-stimulation injections and Kourtney would start hormone injections. Our medicines were mailed to us from a special fertility pharmacy. The

contents of the boxes made us appear as if we were running an illegal drug operation. Needles ranged from cute
and dainty to "Run, she has an ice pick!"

There were all types of vials containing liquids of vary-
ing viscosities. Thankfully, I got the runny, easily inject-
able kind that required using the small needles, similar to
those a diabetic would use. Kourtney was not so lucky. She
received a vial of something as thick as molasses, which had
to be injected into her hindquarters with the giant needle.

She was less than thrilled. "This is not fair. I have to give
myself shots in the butt with horse needles filled with syrup.
You get those stupid dinky ones."

"It can't be that bad," I said. That came from someone
who had never injected herself with anything.

For some reason, Kourtney didn't appreciate my offer
to help her after I shared an anecdote about my one and
only experience with giving shots. "I've done this before. I
could help you. I injected my dad in his arm once. I was so
nervous. I poked the needle in his arm and started to push
the plunger, but it slipped out of my hand and just dangled
from his arm. I eventually got the medicine in."

"I'll pass! Nathan has experience injecting cows. It
can't be much different."

I snickered.

"Oh, shut up! You know what I meant."

I probably should not have given Kourtney a hard time.
Karma bit me and bit hard. The first evening I injected
myself turned into a sitcom for my husband and daughter.
As I unwrapped one of my syringes, I became conscious of

my increased respiration rate. Sweat beads trickled down my head. My hands started shaking as I put the needle into the rubber top of the vial. It wouldn't go in. I tried pushing it in quicker, but I missed the rubber and bent the needle on the metal band.

The second try was better, until it was time to stick it in my abdomen. I wiped myself with a cool alcohol pad until all of its moisture had evaporated. I flicked the syringe as I had seen nurses do, in order to get the air bubbles out. I pushed the air out with the plunger. Not only did all of the air come out but so did half of the medicine.

I let Cedric do the honors of refilling the syringe and removing the air bubbles the third time. He handed it back to me. I wiped my skin and grabbed a fistful of my flesh again. I thought that maybe if I injected it really fast, it wouldn't be as scary. I brought the needle toward my belly, but my hand froze just as I barely pricked myself. I couldn't insert the needle any farther. I tried again and again and was met with an even greater amount of resistance each time.

"Mom, just do it!" Kate screamed. "I want to see!"

"Just be quiet!" I hollered.

I repositioned the syringe in my hand as if I were going to violently stab something with a knife. I stuck it in as fast I could and pushed the medicine. I was either having a hot flash or a panic attack, because I started sweating profusely. I got so hot so quick; I thought I was on fire. I yanked the needle out and caught my breath. After the shock was over, I called Kourtney to ask how her injection went.

"I had to inject this thick oily junk into my ass! It hurts so bad! I tried to do it myself, but I couldn't. Nathan had to. The medicine is so thick; it takes forever to inject. It's horrible!"

Her disdain toward the injections was quite evident. I was just glad I didn't have the same gauge of needle and thick medicine that she did. However, my reaction to my own injection didn't exactly qualify me for an award for bravery.

I kind of felt sorry for her, but it had to be done. I was concerned about the pain it had caused her. Maybe it was too unbearable, and she would refuse to do any more injections. I tried to encourage her the best I could, but even I was not excited about injecting myself every night.

"We won't have to do this forever," I said. "It will be over before we know it. We have to think about the prize at the end. Thank you for doing this for us. You have no idea how much this means to us."

Three days later, Kourtney had blood work done and did the mock embryo transfer. It allowed her to experience what the real transfer would feel like, and it gave the doctor an idea of where to implant the embryos.

"The doctor said it went exactly as it should. I didn't feel a thing."

Whew! I was glad she was in better spirits, after her negative experience with the injections.

"He knows where he wants to implant the embryos. He said I was looking good and on schedule for implantation in a few weeks."

"A few weeks? I never thought I would hear that! It's getting close!" I said.

"I hope I can get pregnant on the first try, because I'm not sure how long I can put up with these injections."

I prayed that we were successful on the first attempt as well. It was going to be a big burden financially if we weren't. I wasn't sure how my mental and emotional state would hold up, either. Hearing Kourtney complain after only three days of injections was discouraging. I understood that she was experiencing pain, but it was bound to get worse if she got pregnant. If I could have traded places with her, I would have. I had learned the hard way what a blessing pregnancy was. What was she going to be like at six months' gestation? She had never faced a long, difficult pregnancy or the loss of a living, breathing child.

I hoped she didn't lose sight of where I was coming from and how important the surrogacy was to me. I buried my hurt feelings and spit out the taste of resentment that was forming in my mouth. I did not want to offend her when we were less than a month away from implantation.

seventeen

Making Babies

June 5, 2011, marked one year since Samuel's death. Coincidentally, that was about the time I started to make daily trips to the doctor to check my hormone levels and egg development. Waking up with the sun and traveling two and a half hours to the fertility clinic gave me plenty of time to fantasize and reminisce. Each new dawn meant I was another day closer to being a mom again. I often thought about what it would be like to hold another baby of my own—the cooing, the tiny fingers and toes, the soft unblemished skin, and the smell of fresh baby powder. My heart palpitated as I thought of what could be. And Samuel maintained a strong hold on my mind and heart. He would have been a year old: walking, talking, waving, and snuggling. My time with him was fleeting and the memories were few, but the pain I felt after losing him was forever ingrained in my soul. A mother never forgets.

Every day for nearly two weeks, my mornings began with a blood draw and evenings ended with a call from the nurse, advising me to change the dosage of my injections so that it would be the ideal amount for the maturing eggs.

One particular evening, I never received a call. I assumed I didn't need to change dosage levels, so I proceeded with my injection and went to bed. The next morning, as I prepared a bagel for breakfast, my phone beeped, indicating that I had a message. On checking it, I felt nauseated and broke down in tears. It was a message from the nurse. The doctor had wanted me to increase my dosage the night before. The nurse had left the message in the afternoon, but due to a poor signal it had hung out in space until the morning.

I was devastated. I had completely messed up any chance for the process to continue. We were going to have to start over. I called the nurse in a panic. "I didn't get your message until this morning. I didn't increase the dosage. I have screwed this up, haven't I?"

"Your eggs are close to maturity anyway. One dose *probably* isn't going to mess things up. Come in for your blood work, and we'll go from there."

I raced to the clinic as if my speed could make my mistake reverse itself. I cried hysterically the entire way. The nurse took my blood, and I left in shambles a few minutes later. I waited by the phone all day, making sure I stayed in locations with a full cellular signal.

I begged God, asking him to make it okay. "Please let this be your will. Please let this happen."

After hours of unbearable waiting, the phone rang. "Hey, this is Lisa. The doctor wants you to reduce the injections. Your estrogen levels are running higher than he thought. It was a good thing you didn't increase your dosage last night."

The tears flowed. *Thank you, God!* I thought as I pumped my fist with excitement.

"The doctor wants you to do an HCG trigger shot tomorrow. This lets the eggs release, just like during ovulation. He will manually retrieve them two days later."

"Thank you so much! I am so relieved."

"You're almost there!"

When I got off the phone, I reached up toward the sky, thanking God and crying unintelligible praises to him. I must have looked crazy, talking aloud to myself, but I didn't care. God was the only one capable of manipulating so many pieces of a puzzle.

The next morning, I prepared myself for my final injection. It took me half an hour to get my nerve up. I stood there panting while the needle barely touched my skin. The previous year flashed before me. In a blink, we had gone from being grieving parents after a traumatic pregnancy to intended parents in a surrogacy.

I pushed the needle into my abdomen and prayed for a perfect egg retrieval, a perfect number of embryos, and a perfect pregnancy on the first attempt. The liquid drained from the syringe, and the physical part of my journey was nearing completion. God, I pray it all goes well. I pray we have the exact number of embryos you want us to have.

We were not going to discard any babies, but I had a horrible fear in the back of my mind that we would have more than we could afford. Finding more women in Oklahoma to do a surrogacy would be a challenge. Then again, Kourtney had fallen in our laps. It was impossible to know what would happen in the future. I really hoped for only two embryos who would survive to be our babies. God had figured it out up to that point; I didn't anticipate his going on a hiatus after the egg retrieval.

Two days later, we made an early morning trip to the clinic where the retrieval would take place. Several rooms in the back were sterile and equipped for more invasive procedures, such as mine. I was prepped just as one would be for surgery. I sported a fashionable gown, a pair of cartoon socks, an IV, a pulse-oxygen monitor, and a few other medical accessories.

There was very little time to think. I was already tired from the early wake-up, and the anesthesiologist had placed the laughing gas mask on my face while the nurse explained the procedure. I started to relax and didn't really focus on her, but whatever she said was quite funny. I was wheeled on a gurney into the operating room and surrounded by a host of medical personnel. I saw my doctor just before the anesthesiologist administered the medicine to put me to sleep.

I giggled uncontrollably. "Hey! I have a new name for you."

"Oh, really. What is that?"

"You are an egg suckin' baby maker," I slurred.

I woke up about forty minutes later in the room I had been prepped in. I was groggy and sore. The nurse, the anesthesiologist, and Cedric were sitting around me.

"Are you awake?" the nurse asked.

"Kind of."

"The doctor was able to retrieve twenty-two eggs. The embryologist will look at their quality and determine how many to fertilize."

The number twenty-two brought me to attention. "Twenty-two? They fertilized twenty-two eggs?"

"Oh, no, no!" she exclaimed. "He hasn't fertilized any. The embryologist will select the best eggs and fertilize those. That number is yet to be determined. Some of the eggs will be poor quality, and those are discarded. He will select only the very best out of the remaining eggs to fertilize. We'll let you know how many that is before it happens. The decision is up to you how many to fertilize."

"Can we just fertilize two?" I asked.

"You can, but the odds of one being able to thrive during the five-day growth period before the transfer into Kourtney are slim. It's better to fertilize more than you think you want."

God, please reduce the egg number, I thought.

I rested at the clinic for a while and then headed home to wait for word about the eggs. I slept away most of the afternoon, which was better than worrying about something out of my control.

We finally received a call from the nurse: "You have sixteen good eggs. You make good, healthy eggs! The doctor thinks fertilizing nine would give you a good chance at getting several healthy embryos. What do you think?"

Nine was an awful lot. I cringed at the thought of having to find surrogates for nine embryos—*impossible.*

"Let me talk to Cedric real quick," I said to her.

I covered the receiver of the phone and squealed, "Cedric! Cedric!"

"What? What are you yelling about?"

"They want to fertilize nine eggs! What do we do?"

"Why so many?" he asked.

"She said it gives us the best chance to get several embryos that are good. That way, if the first implantation doesn't work, we can use any stored embryos and bypass another egg retrieval and fertilization."

"What if all nine make it? What then? We can't afford that!"

"I know, but what if they only fertilize two and they don't survive in Kourtney? We'd have to start all over with the injections and exams, invest more money, and still might face the same scenario of how many eggs to fertilize."

He was in deep thought, processing all I had said. Fertilizing nine eggs was a risk.

"Okay. Tell them to do it," he finally said.

I took a deep breath. "Lisa, let's do it. Fertilize nine."

"Okay, great. I'll call you tomorrow and let you know the results from the first day of growth."

I wasn't superstitious (much), but I crossed my fingers and hoped for lucky number two or *maybe* four. With a total of four, we could try again if the initial implantation failed. Kourtney and I had agreed that only two embryos would be implanted on the first attempt—that was the average number.

I called Kourtney to complain to her. She wasn't sympathetic. In fact, she cracked jokes at my expense. I probably deserved it, having given her a hard time about the injections.

"What if you have all nine? Good thing you live in a big house. You could pay for all of them with your own TV show," she teased.

"I'm giving you half of them if that happens!"

Griping wasn't going to change anything. I tossed and turned all night, tormented over the possibility of nine kids, plus the one we already had. *God, please only give us two to four.*

I waited all the next day for the call. When it came, I was not thrilled about what Lisa had to say.

"The good news is that the fertilization process was successful," she said with more enthusiasm than I was comfortable with. "What may be the shocking news is that all nine were fertilized. It is sort of a rare occurrence!"

Again with the enthusiasm.

"What? Are you serious? All nine?" I felt nauseated.

"Yeah. This is only the first day, though. The embryos will be allowed to grow for several more days. If they make it to day five, they are considered viable. Many stop growing before then. They are not living. The good ones will be implanted or frozen, if there are extra. It's wait and see."

I was a little sad, thinking some of the babies might die, but I was also disturbed that all nine might survive the five days. It was quite a paradox. I went to a quiet place in the house (the bathroom), fell to my knees, and begged God to give us only four at the most.

I found Cedric soon after my petition to God and broke the news to him.

"Are you joking?" he asked, turning pale as if about to be sick. I shook my head. He rubbed his hands through his hair, as he had a tendency to do when he was frustrated. "We'll just deal with it somehow, but I don't know how."

The situation had turned bittersweet. On one hand, I was ecstatic that we had fertilized eggs. On the other hand, I feared we would end up financing multiple surrogates and many more children, because we intended to store any embryos that remained after the implantation.

The tension of the next few days exhausted me. Lisa called on the third day to tell us the embryos were still growing, and implantation would take place in two days. When the fifth and final day of waiting finally came, Kourtney, Nathan, Cedric, and I met at the clinic for the embryo transfer. While together in one room, we discussed the past, the present, and the future. Cedric and I wondered how many embryos had survived. What if they all had suddenly died? Would we even get a chance at a baby? What would we do if all nine survived? Opposing forces were hard at work on us.

Kourtney had her own uncertainties. She had previously expressed, many times, her frustration with the injections. I wasn't too certain she would want to start the process over.

"I hope it wasn't all for nothing," she said. "We had to stop at a nasty convenience store bathroom, so I could put in a suppository that the doctor said had to be inserted exactly two hours before the procedure. I was afraid to touch anything and contaminate myself."

I laughed but totally agreed. I hoped it wasn't all for nothing too. No one in her right mind subjects herself to physical discomfort once she figures out the source. I hated my injections, the daily blood work, and the two-and-a-half-hour drives. I was glad I was done. If Kourtney volunteered to do this a second or third time, she was either a nut or a saint.

The nurse and the doctor came into the room. "It's baby day. Are you all ready for this?" he asked.

Nervous nods and yeses came from around the room.

"How many are there?" I asked. I held my breath, dreading his response.

"Out of the nine fertilized embryos, only four survived to the fifth day. The others stopped developing and are not viable."

Thank you, God. "Whew! I didn't know how we would handle nine more kids. We weren't going to throw embryos away."

Having struggled with pregnancy and wanting a baby for so long, I felt very guilty for being happy they didn't all survive. However, I took into consideration that I had prayed about it and knew God's will would be done. Regardless of the number, I wanted to make sure they didn't throw away live embryos.

I asked the doctor one more time, "Are you sure the others didn't survive? They are not live babies?"

"That's right," said the doctor. "Now, we'd better get started. Lisa will get Kourtney prepped, and we will move over to the sterile room. The embryologist will have the embryos ready. I'll use a catheter to implant two embryos into her uterus, and the other two will be frozen and stored. Kourtney, you will need to take it easy the next few days."

Everyone snickered when Kourtney asked, "Do I need to elevate my butt or anything?"

"No," he said. "You can lie down normally. You'll continue to do your injections until the second trimester—that is, if the embryos stay implanted. We will do a blood test to test for pregnancy in about two weeks. If your hormone levels are on the rise, that is a good sign the embryos attached and you are pregnant."

In the sterile room, Kourtney had to lie down on a table with her feet in stirrups. Because I was barely comfortable with seeing my own naked body in front of a mirror, I made sure there was plenty of distance and bed sheet between Kourtney and me.

A man who looked like an actor in a science fiction movie came into the room wearing a space suit, carrying something in his hand. I could only assume it was the embryologist with our embryos. He handed the container to the doctor, and with a few pokes and prods, the procedure was over.

It was all so exciting and stressful. We had waited for that moment almost a year. Now, there was a whole different waiting game on the horizon. I knew the various milestones that expecting parents anticipated in a pregnancy, but I could only bear to think about one day at a time. I didn't want to hope too much and then have it all squashed by a failed attempt.

Neither Kourtney nor I was patient, because she started taking pregnancy tests soon after the implantation. I only encouraged her by buying more. The first test was negative, which didn't surprise me. It had been only four days. The information I had read was that the earliest a test could be positive was about seven days.

I read blog after blog by disappointed women who had invested their money, time, and hearts in IVF, and it had failed them. I was dejected, thinking I could be one of those women, and it quite possibly was the end of the road. I could only send tearful prayers to God, asking for the blessing of more children.

Two more days passed after the first negative test. Then Kourtney called me on June 26.

"You want to know something?" she asked. I was expecting bad news by her curt tone.

"What's up? Is . . . um . . . is there a problem?"

"Yes. As a matter of fact, there is."

I was about to break down when she quickly changed her gruff demeanor to one of excitement.

"I am . . . I mean . . . you are . . . you're pregnant!"

"What! You're for real! It's positive! For sure?"

She laughed. "Yep! I took two tests. Both positive."

"Yes! Praise God!"

I hollered at Cedric, "She's pregnant! She's pregnant! The test was positive!"

"I gotta go!" I told her. "I need to call people!"

"Okay! Congratulations!"

"Thank you so much!"

Cedric and I embraced. Through our joyful tears, we praised God. "Thank you, God! Thank you!"

The next thing I did was call Diane, the instigator of the surrogacy melee. "She is pregnant!" I exclaimed.

"Yes, yes, yes!" she screamed. "You better be thanking God!"

"We did!"

"This is awesome!"

"I know, right!"

Many couples, including ourselves in past pregnancies, often didn't tell people right away. I wasn't going to wait for an official blood test or an ultrasound, though. I wanted everyone to know and start praying for the pregnancy. They had all supported us during our darkest hours; they deserved to share in this long-awaited miracle.

eighteen

The Pitfalls of Pregnancy

Our fertility doctor scheduled a blood test for the first of July that would verify the home pregnancy test. Kourtney went by herself and later called to tell me that it was positive, but there was some uncertainty. The progesterone hormone that supported pregnancy was lower than expected. Because she was only two or three weeks pregnant, the doctor wasn't concerned; however, it needed to be watched.

"He told me that the progesterone should rise with each blood test. If it doesn't, it might mean I am miscarrying. I'm getting tested again after the holiday weekend. I have felt pretty good so far. I'm usually really sick starting the very first day I get pregnant. I don't know if it's good or bad that I am feeling fine."

I prepared myself for bad news that might come in the near future. So many times, my emotions had been flipped like a switch: happy and hopeful one minute, depressed and angry the next. The news Kourtney had just given me was one of those times. I gave up and went into grieving mode. I knew I shouldn't have hoped. With our history, I should have expected disappointment.

Children were a gift from God, and I was perplexed by the fact that he gave children to people who abused them and treated them like garbage. And many times, people such as Cedric and me, who wanted to care for a child, got nothing but heartache. Yes, we got the guarantee of eternal salvation, which was not taken lightly. Sometimes, however, it was hard to fathom how infinitely better heaven was supposed to be than earth. It was frustrating to hear people say that God worked things out for a greater good, especially when they had never experienced the loss of a child. At the time, in my short-sighted thinking, I reckoned I could achieve satisfaction only through an earthly reward. I wanted another child as payback for my loyalty to Christ, rather than having to wait for my eternal reward. It was difficult to maintain allegiance to my heavenly father when faced with difficulty over and over again.

I remembered a cliché that many Christians used: "There is a God-shaped hole in all of us." Well, there was a baby-shaped hole in me. I certainly loved God, but he made me very depressed sometimes. I had a void that needed to be filled with a child. Ironically, only he could make it happen.

Once I finished sulking about the direction the pregnancy was heading, I managed to swing back to happiness and prepared for the neighborhood Independence Day celebration. We invited Kourtney and her family to the gathering. It was a big deal. I had been a teen when the neighbors and my family first got together to have some Fourth of July fun. We had been having the event for fifteen years. I wanted everyone in my circle to meet the mystery woman who carried our babies.

At the party, sixty curious guests surrounded Kourtney and me to ask questions. No one knew much about surrogacy. Some had never even heard the term *surrogacy.* They were conservative country folk and mostly isolated themselves from progressive concepts. The closest thing to surrogacy they ever experienced was transferring embryos between cows. It was the same idea, only different animals. Yet I could never complain about the level of support Cedric and I had received before and after Samuel's death, so I had no doubt they would support us during Kourtney's pregnancy with our children.

The very next day, Kourtney, her two kids, Kate, and I drove to the doctor to get a second blood test. The drive was nerve-wracking for me on multiple levels. I was worried about what the results would reveal about the pregnancy, but I was more concerned about getting us there safely with obnoxious, screaming children who were kicking the backs of the seats. Kate (six), Lilly (four), and Jace (two) filled the entire back seat of my small car. Kate, who should have been the most mature child, was complaining the loudest. She was stuck in the middle of two booster seats. Jace was on one side of her, pulling fists full of hair from her tender head, and Lilly was on the other side, playing twenty questions with the *older* girl who sat next to her.

"Mom! Jace is pulling out all my hair, and Lilly is bothering me."

Kourtney and I laughed. I had a flashback to my younger days when my siblings and I shared the back seat of our giant Buick. I remembered being just as loud and quarrelsome. Those were the days when my mother carried a flyswatter, and my father had his huge hand to keep us in check.

"You'd better get used to it, Kate," said Kourtney. "You might have a brother *and* a sister on the way."

I had a lot to get used to myself. I hadn't been around babies in a while. When Kourtney went into the fertility clinic for her blood work, I stayed in the car with the kids. Jace decided to break me in with a leaky diaper. I sat him in the front seat, which sort of reclined, but not enough. He had to sit up while I awkwardly maneuvered the clean diaper into place. He looked at me with scorn, as if saying, "You are an idiot." At least he was gracious enough not to pee in my face or on the seat.

After the brief visit to the clinic, we stopped for a bite to eat. I didn't think my car would ever be the same after the three kids ate their meals like wild hyenas. Jace threw his "mean beans" (green beans) everywhere, Lilly dumped her drink on the floor, and Kate managed to spread her chicken crumbs all over the seat. I looked in the rear-view mirror and shook my head.

"Are you ready for this?" Kourtney asked, failing to hold back her giggles.

"I might not have a choice." I had to admit that Kate, Lilly, and Jace were more than I could bear for much longer.

I didn't know how Kourtney was going to function with her two kids while my two kids tormented her body from the inside out. There were times when she exhibited her frustration with her own kids during our trip. How would her stress be magnified by her kids' demands in the late stages of pregnancy? How was that stress going to affect my babies? I worried that her kids might increase that level of anxiety beyond what my unborn children could tolerate. What if the doctor restricted her lifting capabilities? Would she follow orders and not lift her forty-pound child? Could I really trust her? I remembered not being able to lift Kate when I was on bed rest; it was so painful to see her upset about something and be unable to scoop her up in my arms and console her.

I wasn't sure whether Kourtney—or any woman, for that matter—had it in her not to mother her own children for the sake of mine. In my mind, the welfare of my unborn children was the most important issue. Selfish? Absolutely. What parents would not do everything in their power to protect their children?

I dropped Kourtney and her kids off at their house. Then Kate and I headed to a family gathering. It was the last time we would have all of our kids together. Had I known that at the time, I would have cherished the loud squeals coming from the back and the green beans thrown into the front.

By early evening, I had almost arrived at my destination. Just as I stopped for supper, I received a call from Kourtney. "You'd better get ready for more craziness,

because the second blood test is positive, and my progesterone is much higher. It's safe to say I am preggo!"

"Yes! Oh, Lord. Yes! I'm going to cry now. I need to go."

"Thank you, Jesus!" I screamed through my tears.

Kate was in the back seat, engrossed in a video game
and unfazed by my zealous reaction to the news. I let her
enjoy her alone time—she would be sharing it *and* the
video game in the future. I didn't really want to get her
hopes up anyway. I had always felt guilty for not being able
to give her a sibling. We had shielded her from the grief of
our own previous losses. She always knew she had broth-
ers and a sister who had died during birth, but we mostly
stayed mute. We did the same thing with the surrogacy; we
made an effort not to get her too involved, hoping that
it preserved her feelings. Cedric and I were both keenly
aware of the emotional toll that the loss of a child could
take on a person.

Up to that point, the surrogacy was actually more stressful than being pregnant myself. An endless amount of time
would have to pass before we had a baby in our arms, so I
remained guarded. I expected many more peaks and val-
leys; this would most likely be the trend for the duration
of the pregnancy. I had failed miserably at handling the
minor hiccups; I hated to think what kind of psychotic
state I might be in if something major occurred. God
hadn't made the surrogacy easy so far. Things were working out, but it hadn't been hassle-free. I was sure I would go
through more crying, begging, pleading, and questioning.
I was certain to experience more mixed feelings during the

journey. Through it all, God would still be God, regardless of my tantrums. And in my heart, I knew God was good.

We faced another valley two days after the positive blood test. Kourtney texted: I'M SPOTTING. NOT A LOT. WHAT DO YOU WANT ME TO DO?

My heart hurt. I texted back: CALL THE DOCTOR!

I didn't have any explanations for her. Many women had some sort of bleeding during pregnancy. In most cases, it didn't mean anything bad (unless the woman was me). I angrily called out to God, "Why should I expect normal from you? You never gave me normal! I hate being out of control. Just watch over them, please."

Kourtney touched base with the doctor and then me. "He said it's more common to spot in IVF pregnancies."

Apparently, he wasn't concerned, but I was.

"Well, spotting wasn't normal for me," I said. "So, okay. Whatever!"

Thank goodness for our annual trip to Florida. I figured that leaving to do something fun for a few days would cool me off. Who was I kidding? I was wound too tight. Leaving exacerbated issues, because being farther away made me feel even more out of control. We were going to miss out on the first ultrasound as well. That wasn't such great planning on my part.

We toured Disney World during the busiest time of the year and in the hottest weather. *So much for chilling out.* The oppressive Florida heat burned our pale skin and sucked the sweat from our bodies, and the humidity zapped every ounce of energy we had acquired from the overpriced ice

cream, soda, and popcorn. Yet we pressed on from one diz-
zying attraction to the next—fingers crossed—and waited
for good news from back home.

During one of our many long marches at Hollywood
Studios, I received a text from an unknown number. There
was only a fuzzy black-and-gray picture. The quality was very
poor, but my motherly heart skipped a beat when I realized
I was looking at two little babies on an ultrasound photo.
They looked like gummy bears; they were our gummy bears.

"Twins!" I yelled to Cedric while we stood in the middle
of the fake street. "They are both there!"

I immediately called Kourtney. She had sent the text
from her husband's phone. I talked ninety miles an hour.
"What did the doctor say? Are they healthy? Are they okay?"

"He said they looked great. The due date would be early
to mid-March, but expect an earlier delivery with multiples."

"What about the spotting?"

"It is barely noticeable. He's not worried."

"Awesome! We'll be home soon. What about you? Are
you feeling okay?"

"Ugh. I've been sick all day with morning sickness. It
sucks. I think it's worse with two."

I couldn't sympathize with her. Morning sickness made
the pregnancy more real, and that made me happy—that
is, until she started in on her blood pressure.

"My blood pressure has been high too. I hope it's not
PIH."

It seemed awfully early for pregnancy-induced hypertension (PIH). That typically happened after twenty weeks'

gestation. PIH was a serious matter; the only way to stop it was to induce labor. Something was amiss.

"Do you need something? Do you need help?"

"No. I am fine!" she said.

She didn't sound fine. She had just told me she had high blood pressure.

"If it gets worse, you should probably go to the hospital," I advised.

"If I lie down, it goes lower. It's usually fine."

She gave me mixed messages, which made me confused and frustrated. Was her blood pressure up or down? I kept my mouth shut. It was no use responding negatively. I didn't have much room to complain anyway. Being unappreciative because I had to deal with a sick pregnant lady who carried my babies would not win me sympathy from anyone. I ended the conversation before I said something I shouldn't.

I was elated that both embryos were thriving. The rest of our vacation was perfect, but on returning home, we paid a visit to the infirmary. Kourtney's blood pressure had remained high, so she went to the emergency room and was admitted to the hospital. We were about eight weeks into the pregnancy and faced a potentially serious problem. I watched the blood pressure monitor, and it was above average but not consistently and not extraordinarily high. It still made me nervous though.

"Well, this is just crap!" I ranted. "You can't stay pregnant if your blood pressure is uncontrollable. The doctors won't let you. They will terminate the pregnancy."

"They gave me some medicine in my IV to control it. It helped, but I don't really want to take it. It made me feel weird."

I gritted my teeth. I was sure that slapping a pregnant lady was frowned upon. "I'll talk to the doctor to see if there is something else she can do."

I walked out and caught the doctor who had been treating Kourtney. As luck would have it, she also served as my general physician. I thought I might be able to sway her into doing something different. *Maybe she can give Kourtney a sedative to put her to sleep for the remainder of the pregnancy, so I don't have to listen to her.*

"Kourtney is unhappy about how the blood pressure medicine is making her feel. Is there anything else you can try?" I asked.

By the doctor's facial expressions and snippy response, it was obvious she and Kourtney had exchanged pleasantries already.

"She is pregnant; there are only so many things to try! She is being given the most effective medicine; the side effects aren't dangerous, just slightly uncomfortable. Her symptoms are normal. I can try one other drug, but it doesn't work as well, and the dosage typically has to be increased the further along a pregnancy gets."

"I'm sorry. I'm not trying to tell you how to do your job. Kourtney is griping to me, so I have to try to do something."

"I get it. We can try this other medicine and go from there. Good luck," she said, rolling her eyes and walking away without another word.

Back in Kourtney's room I went with news that hopefully would be well received. "The doctor is going to try a new medicine with lesser side effects. The downside is that you may have to take more of it to control the blood pressure."

"It's got to be better than what they have given me."

The only real positive note for me was getting to see the babies on ultrasound. Their little hearts beat away. I was so ready to be done with the pregnancy and cuddle them. I had grown weary after only eight weeks; I suspected that these challenges were only the beginning. It was stressful trying to meet someone else's needs.

I wanted to express my feelings bluntly to Kourtney and say, "You did volunteer for this, so shut up and do it!" However, I figured that this reaction might make her angry enough to keep the babies for herself. It was a lost cause. I was in it for the long haul and needed to stay focused on getting the babies safely.

Having stabilized, Kourtney was released after a couple of days with the new blood pressure medicine she would take daily. I bought her a blood pressure monitor so that she could check it more frequently and report back to me. I was thinking it would be helpful and would ease our minds if she monitored it regularly.

I was wrong. As soon as she got home, she texted: IT'S HIGH.

WELL, DID YOU TAKE A PILL YET? I texted back.

NO.

OKAY. TAKE ONE AND LET ME KNOW.

Good grief! Why did things have to be so complex? During my pregnancies, I was able to make decisions for myself in order to find solutions. The surrogacy was like shaking a box of puzzle pieces, trying to get them to fit into place. It was impossible—or at least not very easy—to get someone else to think like me.

If I could have seen into the future, I'm not sure I would have pursued surrogacy. I was so caught up in wanting another baby; I didn't realize I would be giving up what little control I had when it came to making decisions about another person's physical and mental health. God was constantly reminding me that he was bigger than me.

Kourtney called a few hours later. "It's lower but still high for me."

"Maybe the doctor needs to increase the dose. Just lie low for a while and relax."

"I don't know how I'm supposed to do that! My house is a mess, and my kids are always wanting something! Nobody helps me do anything around here! I have to do it all! I'm sick of everything!"

Surely, it was the hormones talking. She seemed to be two seconds away from having a nervous breakdown. She had way too much going on and that included incubating my children. The stress couldn't have been good for anyone. I couldn't assist her, because I was reporting back to school in a couple of days.

"I can't help you, but is there anyone you know who can? Do you have a friend or a relative who doesn't work? We would pay them to help you."

"I can deal with it! This is my house and my kids! I should be able to take care of it!"

"You are obviously stressed. It's not healthy for anyone. Try to find someone. We would be willing to pay $10 an hour for someone to help you cook and clean and care for Lilly and Jace."

She paused for a minute. It was a pretty good offer. She would be getting a nanny and a maid for free. "Okay. I'll ask some people and see if they could come help."

I could hear a sigh of relief in her voice.

It wasn't long before she called me back—with good news, for a change. "My grandma and a friend are willing to help during the day."

"Great. Just write down their hours, and we'll pay them at the end of each week."

Later, it dawned on me that she might not like the arrangement. I knew, being an expert control freak myself, that it was hard to let someone else do things for me. Going from being independent to dependent was a difficult thing for me to accept. Kourtney was no different; she was stubborn and did things a certain way. I hoped she didn't fire the help on the first day. Regardless, it made me feel better if someone else was doing the cooking, cleaning, and chasing after kids, so that she could focus on caring for my babies. The question had been lingering in my mind for a while: "How is she going to juggle her kids and mine?" I couldn't demand that she ignore her kids. I hoped that paying someone to help her would be the solution.

nineteen

Role Reversal

August 8 was the first day Kourtney received assistance with her chores and kids. I was relieved to know that her help would be there, taking care of the bulk of the labor. I felt pretty good about the current state of affairs until she called me about eight o'clock in the morning. I cringed. *What has gone wrong now?*

"Jace is throwing up and crying a lot. I'm taking him to the doctor. Something isn't right."

I wasn't sure why she'd informed me about it. There was nothing earth shattering about a kid vomiting. I didn't think it was a big deal. Then again, I had a phobia about it: if it was me doing the throwing up, it would have been a big deal.

"Do you need help or something?"

"No, my friend is here with me."

I tried to reassure her. "It's probably the stomach flu. Kids run a fever, vomit, and all that fun stuff."

I remained skeptical, however, about Jace's actual condition. I didn't know whether Kourtney was being overly dramatic about his symptoms. I had felt a little burned out during several of our past conversations regarding her blood pressure and other pregnancy issues. She couldn't quite decide whether her blood pressure was high or low, whether she should call the doctor, or if spotting was normal or abnormal. I was concerned about how her physical symptoms affected my babies, and I really wanted to know about any changes—but not imagined ones that led to unnecessary stress.

"So, how's the blood pressure today?" I asked. "Is the medicine working?"

"It's fine. No problems so far."

"Okie dokie. That's good. Keep me posted on Jace."

I shouldn't have been apathetic concerning Jace. I felt bad for him, but I didn't think he was in danger. Nonetheless, I was happy her blood pressure was normal. I didn't give his illness a second thought. I spent the rest of the day relaxing and enjoying the last bit of summer vacation. It was interrupted—but only once—with a text from Kourtney: JACE QUIT THROWING UP, THANKS TO MEDICINE. HE IS VERY LETHARGIC, THOUGH.

I replied: SOUNDS NORMAL TO BE WEAK AFTER BARFING A LOT. HE MAY BE DEHYDRATED. GIVE HIM LIQUIDS. HE'LL PERK BACK UP.

She wrote back: I'VE BEEN HOLDING HIM ALL DAY. I NEED A NAP. LOL!

LET ME KNOW IF YOU NEED SOMETHING, I typed.

I didn't have contact with her again until later that evening. I never dreamed our situation could get any more bizarre. Only God could take two strangers, weave them into one soul for a moment in time, and have them experience each other's trials and heartaches on an almost identical scale. Our roles reversed in a matter of hours.

Diane called me about eight-thirty. She was frantic, breathing so loud and fast I could hardly understand her. "It's . . . it's . . . it's Jace! He's . . . dying! Unresponsive. They're doing CPR. I'm on my way to the ER now!"

"Whoa, what? What's going on? What happened? I talked to Kourtney earlier. He was sick with a stomach bug or something. He was just throwing up."

"They don't know! They don't know! They said he was sick. They took him in. It's bad. He's dying! I'll find out more and call you. Just pray!"

I yelled at Cedric, "Jace is unresponsive! They are doing CPR!"

"What?"

He said something else, but my mind had already been blurred with thoughts of a little boy lying motionless on a gurney while a doctor pounded away on his chest, trying to get life back into him. I was in a state of disbelief. How could it have gotten so bad? I had downplayed it as nothing earlier in the day, but a child was dying. I felt horrible for telling Kourtney it was the stomach flu. I was always super worried when Kate got sick. I should have had more compassion. I felt physically ill. I ran to the back bedroom, hit my knees, and prayed, "My God, please keep him safe. Don't do this to her. She does not need this right now. We don't need this."

I trembled, not knowing what to do and wondering what had happened to Jace.

Diane finally called back with news. "He's gone. It's over."

"No! No! This can't happen. Why? How?"

"They don't know. He's gone . . . he's gone."

As I listened to my dear friend weep over the phone, I began sobbing, which turned into dry heaves. My guilt festered like an open sore. Kourtney, pregnant with my babies, had just lost her own. Jace had turned two years old only two weeks earlier. The death of a child was every mother's worst nightmare. What had God done? How was any good going to come of this? There was no way I would ever be able to talk about the surrogacy again. It seemed so insensitive. When Samuel died, I didn't want to be around children at all. How would Kourtney feel about my babies that she carried or even about me, the soon-to-be mom?

"What should I do?" I asked Diane. "I'm afraid to talk to her. I don't want to upset her or her parents. I don't want her parents to see me and be reminded of the pregnancy. They were against it anyway. They lost a grandson. Maybe they might resent us."

"Why don't you just talk to Kourtney? Explain it to her. She needs support right now."

Diane handed the phone to Kourtney. On hearing her voice, I broke down. I sobbed, "I am so sorry. I can't describe how sorry I am."

"I know. Thanks."

"If you need anything, please let me know. I want to give you space during this time. I don't want to bother you or upset anyone with texts and phone calls. I'll lie low."

"You won't bother me. It's fine, really."

Even in the middle of her tragic situation, she offered *me* hope that things would be okay. "I had the nurse take my blood pressure," she said. "It's alright."

"Please don't worry about the pregnancy. Just forget it and focus on you and your family."

I felt helpless and wanted to do anything to comfort her. I swallowed hard and prepared myself to say something that hurt to even think about; I wanted God to take the breath right out of me. I thought Kourtney might be considering a means to right the wrong that had just happened to her. "I understand if you want to terminate the pregnancy so you can rebuild your own family."

I just bawled. I didn't mean it at all, but I assumed she would want to fix the hole in her heart as soon as possible.

"No! I wouldn't do that," she said. "We'll deal with this. Don't worry about it."

She sounded so calm on the phone. I was the one who was hysterical. Everything suddenly got even more complicated. God didn't seem interested in stopping the ongoing crises that plagued us. What was next? A terminal illness? Another untimely death? Financial ruin? God used circumstances to manifest his power and grace, but why through the death of a child? Why during an already tumultuous time? Cedric and I were too familiar with loss. We didn't need another reminder that we had no control over situations—good or bad. The woman carrying *our* children in her womb had to experience a horrific tragedy. What happened to mercy? Jace's death was almost unconscionable.

I grieved for her, but I worried for my unborn children as well. How would this affect them? Maybe it was God's way of reducing Kourtney's load of two young children and a surrogate pregnancy. I couldn't help but think her loss might have been for my gain. But then again, the agony of losing a child seemed a far greater burden to bear in Kourtney's condition: pregnant with complications. I prayed for Kourtney. I never had the right words for God, though. I offered up only jumbled thoughts. God was such a challenge to love sometimes. I'm sure he thought the same thing about me.

I spoke with Diane the morning after Jace's death and asked her to keep me updated on Kourtney and the funeral arrangements. I knew she would have lots of visitors and family gatherings, and I didn't want to interfere. I wanted her to receive the attention she deserved as a grieving mother. Diane reassured me that Kourtney was still going do everything to keep the babies safe.

"I want you to know that Kourtney is very concerned about the babies," Diane said. "While she was holding Jace after he died, she asked the nurse to check her blood pressure, because she was worried about the welfare of the babies. She won't let anything happen to them. In fact, the babies might be the very thing that she needs to distract her mind. If I know my stubborn niece, she will be on a mission to make this happen."

I was taken aback by Kourtney's selfless actions, despite facing her own crisis. While cradling her dead baby, she was worried about mine. I could never hold a candle to that. I was ashamed of all of the petty things that had upset me in the past.

☙•❧

I made it a priority to visit Kourtney before the funeral. That meant I had to go to her parents' house. I was not real excited about it. Kourtney was sitting outside with her father and Nathan as we pulled up into the driveway. It was the first time we had met her dad and was very similar to my first encounter with her mother. Her father was distant and aloof. Under the circumstances, I wasn't surprised. Anyone who had lost a child in his or her family got a behavior pass in my book. However, it didn't change the fact that I really wanted her parents' approval to end my guilt about *stealing* their daughter's womb for my benefit. I seriously wondered whether they blamed me for the situation. Maybe Kourtney had been too preoccupied with the pregnancy to recognize the gravity of Jace's condition. I anticipated them hating me, because my babies occupied the space that their grandbaby needed.

Talking with a parent who had just lost a child was awkward. It must have been how people felt talking to me. You just don't have the right words to say. I let Kourtney steer the conversation, and Jace was right in the middle of it. "Jace had a tear in his intestine, according to the autopsy. He went into septic shock. It was too late to fix it."

"How did it tear? Was it something he ate?"

"The report said it was Meckel's diverticulum. It's a congenital defect. There is a piece of extra intestine in there—almost like an appendix. A weakness was in the wall of it, apparently."

"I'm sorry," I said, ashamed of my weak response. I had to come up with something better than that so she would know I cared, but I had nothing to say that seemed poetic or creative—or simply meaningful. I tested the waters and tried to talk about happier memories. I reminded her of our last outing with all of the kids. We laughed about Jace pulling Kate's hair and throwing his "mean beans." That was the one and only thing I could share. I had not interacted with him very much. Our history consisted of an awkward diaper change, wads of hair, and vegetables, but it was enough to get Kourtney to smile and proved that the simple moments of life can leave lasting impressions.

A few days later, we attended Jace's funeral. It was . . . well . . . a child's funeral. It was nice, if you can say that about a funeral. The words *child* and *funeral* shouldn't have to be used in the same sentence. It was unnatural and went against what our brains were programmed to expect: birth, aging, and then death. When I was a child growing up, it never seemed as if those rules were broken. My parents sheltered me from anything that was out of the ordinary. I assume it maintained my innocence. Not until I got older did I realize life was so fleeting.

At the cemetery, I nervously waited my turn to give condolences to the family: Nathan, Kourtney, and both sets of their parents. I feared negative interactions with the latter. The first person to greet me was Kourtney's mom. I hated hugging, but everyone in line ahead of me was doing it, so I was trapped. I cautiously extended my arms, and much to my chagrin, Kourtney's mom latched on and didn't let go.

"I'm very sorry," I whispered, due to her constricting arms wrapped around me. I expected the standard answer, "Thanks for coming."

Nope. I was blown away when she cried and said, "I want to hear about Samuel, someday."

I acknowledged her comment with a dumbfounded look and moved on to the next person, with her statement burned into my mind. It was as if a noose had been loosened from my neck; I could breathe again. She had extended her empathetic hand and made a peace offering, of sorts—not that there had been hostility earlier. In fact, we had interacted very little. It was the standoffishness that bothered me more than anything else.

I wished our families hadn't been forced to meet on the common ground of a child's death. I knew that hard times would soon follow. It was merely the beginning of their pain, sadness, anger, frustration, emptiness, and confusion. God made no mistakes, though. It was apparent that my role in the surrogate pregnancy was more than being a new mother—that was just a perk. I knew in my soul that it was God's desire for me to be a friend to Kourtney, to empathize with her, and to share the burden of losing her son. I would have chosen a different track, but I was equipped with God-given tools to help her, just as God had equipped her to help me. Our paths had not crossed by chance; they were made to intersect by our omnipotent God.

Kourtney didn't stay out of touch for very long. It was maybe a couple of days after the funeral when she made contact with me. I had told her I would keep my distance, because I thought she would need time to absorb everything and begin the healing process. Not Kourtney. She couldn't resist the lure of the text message. I figured that this meant she was ready to get back on the horse.

She texted: THESE BABIES ARE MAKING ME HUNGRY. LOL.

Her resiliency amazed me. It bewildered me, though, that she was so candid so soon after her son's death. In fact, I hadn't seen her break down and cry, even at the funeral. She was either very strong or a great actress. I was not sending humorous texts to people after Samuel passed away. I had isolated myself from the rest of the world and grieved. I assumed that maybe her coping mechanism was opposite of mine; she needed people. I figured I should accommodate her and respond in a way that reflected what she was saying or feeling in any given moment. I sent an amusing text of my own.

NOM, NOM, NOM!

She sent me back a smiley face. It felt good not to be so solemn, and it seemed as if we had our first breakthrough. It was the start of another new normal—*ish.*

twenty

Jace's Gift

I suppose it was wrong to presume that God subjects any given person to only a limited amount of difficulty. I'd figured that miscarriages and dead children were as challenging as God was going to be.

About a week after Jace's death, Kate fell ill. While visiting with Diane one evening, Kate complained of back pain. I was very concerned, because I thought it might be a kidney infection. She had a congenital condition that left her predisposed to that ailment. I made a run to the local pharmacy and bought an over-the-counter kit to test for infection in the urinary tract. The test was negative. This gave me a little bit of reassurance, so I figured her pain must have been caused by a strained muscle or another minor thing. When we got home, I gave her some ibuprofen and a warm bath and sent her to bed.

The next day all was well, so my anxiety subsided. After church, though, she complained of more pain. First it was in her back, and then it moved to her stomach. I feared that my hypochondriac tendencies were rubbing off on her, and she was imagining sicknesses—the imaginary ones were always worse than the real ones. I quizzed her to determine what was going on. "Is your back still hurting?"

"No. Just my stomach."

"Are you hungry?"

"No. I feel sick thinking about it."

Kate was not a complainer. She was a kid who would throw up and then ask for a cookie.

"Have you pooped today?" I asked.

"Mom! No!"

"Maybe you are constipated."

"My stomach just hurts."

"Where does it hurt?"

"Over here," she said, pointing to the right. The location of the pain threw up red flags. I knew anatomy well enough to realize it might be her appendix. I checked her temperature; she had a slight fever. I took some time to research medical websites. She had a few symptoms, but they didn't scream appendicitis.

"On a scale of one to ten, how bad does it hurt?" I asked.

"Five."

That was just average. Typically, people with appendix issues were in more pain, had higher fevers, and were vomiting. My head said one thing, but my gut said another. In the back of my mind was Jace. I replayed the day he died; it had gone from nothing to catastrophe in mere hours. I hated to be an alarmist. I didn't want to take her to the clinic if it was only a stomach ache.

Doctors always had a way of making one feel stupid when that happened. I wanted to test her to see how bad she was.

"I'm taking you to the emergency room, and they might make you stay."

"Okay. I want to go," she said.

Huh? I was shocked. She must have been really sick to want to go to a hospital. I knew she had seen me in them enough that she hated them. In addition to her response, something else urged me to get her examined. Maybe it was paranoia, but I wasn't willing to wait around to find out.

We drove twenty minutes to the nearest hospital. I called Cedric to give him an update.

"Kate's sick. She isn't acting right. I think it's her appendix."

"It's probably nothing. You're just paranoid. Let me know," he said. "I'm sure she is fine."

He never got too excited about medical events. I handled that for both of us.

After I checked Kate in, we went to the restroom to see whether she could get any relief before we had to fork over $1,000.

"I feel a little better," she said.

"Whew! Good deal. I told you it was just constipation." I was so proud of the fact I had made that diagnosis earlier.

As we were about to exit the hospital to go home, she got a funny look on her face.

"I need to barf!" she said, covering her mouth.

"Run to the bathroom!" I yelled.

She vigorously shook her head no.

"I need a vomit bag!" I called out to the receptionist.

She grabbed a blue plastic bag from the wall dispenser, shoved it to me, and I put it in Kate's face just before the barfing commenced. I turned to the receptionist and said, "You can add throwing up to the list of symptoms."

"Do you feel better?" I asked Kate.

"No, my stomach still hurts."

I got even more anxious, so I called Diane for reinforcement. I didn't want to be alone, just in case things got bad. "Can you come to the ER? Kate is sick. I think it might be her appendix."

"I'm on my way."

Diane lived only a few blocks away, and I was so relieved when she arrived.

After a several-hour wait, Kate was called back to see the doctor. I immediately expressed my concern about appendicitis.

"We'll do some blood work and an X-ray," he said. He sat down beside Kate's bed. "I'm going to push on your stomach. You tell me where it hurts."

She giggled as he pressed his hand on her abdomen. "That tickles," she said.

He glared back at me. "Kids with appendicitis are very sick. Considering she is laughing, I don't suspect anything major here. If anything, it is maybe a virus. I'll still run tests for your peace of mind."

Once he left, I scolded Kate. "You can't laugh! Now he thinks you are faking something." Even I had my doubts, but Jace's death and my maternal instinct said otherwise. I looked to Diane for an answer as Kate went for her X-ray and blood work.

"What do you think?" I asked.

She shrugged her shoulders. "I'm not sure. She was laughing, but she looks *so* pale and has dark circles under her eyes."

After Kate completed her tests, we waited another hour before the doctor came back in with the results.

He smirked. "Just as I thought. Her white cell count is barely elevated. She has a virus and will be fine in a few days."

We left for home, but I was uneasy about the doctor's diagnosis. His bedside manner had really irritated me, but something else was driving my distrust. My mind was over-run with thoughts of Jace. The circumstances surrounding his death were rare, but it still scared me. He had also been to the doctor. I knew my child. She wasn't acting the same as she had in the past when she was sick with normal kid stuff.

I made her get into the bathtub to relax while I talked to Cedric, who had arrived home from work. He was satis-fied with the doctor's report and told me to let well enough alone. Then I heard Kate hollering, "Mooom! My stomach still hurts."

I scowled at Cedric. "She's not fine. Something is wrong. Think of what happened to Jace."

"Oh, you always think the worst!"

"Well, you can sleep on the couch tonight while I monitor her," I said, disgruntled at his nonchalance.

We went to bed around ten, but we did not go to sleep. Kate tossed and turned and moaned for two hours. I'd had enough. I woke Cedric up, then called our family doctor. "She is feverish, vomited earlier today, and has pain on her right side. We already went to one emergency room. I don't want to be embarrassed at the other one as well. What do I do?"

"I'm telling you," the doctor said, "I think she has appendicitis. You can do one of two things. Go to the other ER in town, and I'll order some tests. Another option is to go to the pediatric hospital, but it's a couple-hour drive and a really long wait to see a physician."

I cringed at the thought of going to the other local hospital. That was where Jace had taken his final breath. However, I didn't want Kate's situation to get worse if we had to drive and then wait for hours to see a doctor.

"Okay. We'll go to the local one, I guess."

"I'll make sure they are ready for you," she said.

At one in the morning, back to town we went. Cedric shared his disapproval. "The only reason I'm doing this is because of Jace. I don't think there is a problem."

"There is something," I said. "I can feel it."

As soon as we checked in, the nurse called us to the back. "Your doctor ordered a CT scan with contrast dye. Kate has to ingest the dye, so we can get a good picture of her insides. If your daughter has appendicitis, we will know for sure."

Getting Kate to drink the banana-flavored liquid chalk was a big challenge—nearly impossible. Out of frustration, I threatened her, "Drink it or you will get a whipping!"

I feared for her life, so I had no choice. Coaxing her hadn't worked. She was still at the age where corporal punishment from Mom was scary, so she choked down the disgusting concoction.

I paced the floor while she went to get the CT scan. My nerves were shot. I had flashbacks to Jace's death. Diane had shown me pictures of Kourtney holding him. He had been dressed in a child-size gown covered with cartoon drawings of sleeping tiger cubs. Now Kate was wearing an identical gown. It wasn't right that gowns were made that small—to fit our innocent babies. I wondered whether we were in the same room where they had worked on Jace, trying to get his little heart beating again. I shook with terror as I envisioned myself holding Kate's lifeless body, just as Kourtney had held her son's.

Cedric and the nurse wheeled Kate back into the room.

"We'll have the results in an hour or so," the nurse said.

I tried to rest, but it was useless. I feared that God was going to take my only child away from me. She lay in a hospital bed, and there was nothing I could do. I imagined that Kourtney had experienced the same helpless feeling as she watched her child die.

After a long wait (well over an hour), the doctor reported back to us. "Kate's appendix is definitely inflamed, but it has not ruptured yet. She needs an appendectomy now. We can't do it, because she doesn't meet our physical requirements. She's too little. She'll have to ride by ambulance to the pediatric hospital and have surgery there. One of you can ride with her."

I was relieved to know what the problem was; however, surgery on my child was not the most pleasing thought. Things could go wrong during surgery as well. My anxiety skyrocketed. I couldn't deal with it anymore. I looked at Cedric and started sobbing. "You go with her. I can't. I need a break. I'll drive the car and try to calm down."

He gave me a hug. "It will be fine. And just for the record, you are always right."

I wished I hadn't been this time.

"You might want to leave now, because the ambulance will drive faster than you," the doctor said.

We made 3:00 a.m. phone calls to family members and sent texts to others, asking for prayer. I hesitantly texted Kourtney. I was actually afraid to tell her Kate was sick, but that she had a diagnosis and would get well after surgery. There was a moment when I thought Kourtney might be jealous that my child was being saved and hers hadn't been. I'd had those feelings when Samuel had passed away, while other children made it out of the NICU and got to go home. I had never wished ill on those families, but I was envious.

Kourtney didn't respond immediately, but she called later while I was on the road. "What happened?"

I explained everything that had occurred, starting with Kate's back pain at Diane's. "If it wasn't for Jace, we wouldn't have pursued anything. He helped me make the choice to keep going. Otherwise, I don't know what would have happened."

I sped to the hospital but arrived only a few minutes before the ambulance. The doctors and the nurses got Kate situated and gave her pain medicine. It was going to be a few hours until surgery. She must have not been in immediate danger, because the medical personnel didn't seem to be in any hurry to start. We were all exhausted and just wanted it to be over, so we could take our daughter home.

Finally, at 2:00 p.m., nearly two days after Kate had first complained, she was rolled away to the operating room. As we waited in the family area for several hours, I was plagued by the fact I had no control.

On the table next to us sat an old beige-colored phone that rang nonstop. It served as a link between the waiting families and the recovery room nurses, who monitored the children after surgery. Once family members received a call, they could go to the room to see their child. With each ring, I was as startled as if I'd received a call during deep sleep in the dead of night. A shot of adrenaline surged through my body, sending my heart into overdrive. Call after call came for others, but none for us.

As the waiting area crowd thinned, I became more apprehensive. We were one of the last families remaining. I was in desperate need of answers, so I caught the first nurse in the hall whom I saw.

"I need to know how my daughter is. Kate Janzen . . . she has been in surgery for a long time."

"I'll check," she said.

I wondered why we ever wanted more children. It was obvious I couldn't handle situations where children were in fragile states. My heart pounded as the nurse walked toward me. I crossed my arms across my waist and pressed on my stomach, which was in a giant knot. My anxiety-controlled brain expected the worst, so my eyes welled up with tears as she started to speak. The first few words came out of her mouth as if in slow motion.

"She's . . . still . . . sleeping. Surgery . . . went . . . well. One at a time, you can go back to see her."

"What? Really?" I said, surprised that she hadn't said something much more sinister. "She's okay?"

"Yes. She's going to be fine. Go back when you're ready. She should be waking up soon."

I ran back to the waiting area where Cedric was sitting.

"We can go back! She's sleeping, but she's okay," I said, crying tears of joy and relief.

"Thank God! Let's go back."

"We can only go one at a time, and I am going first."

"Okay, go. But hurry back."

I hustled down the hall and buzzed the nurses' station, so they would let me into the recovery area. I was surprised to see Kate in a room with six children, who were also recovering from various surgeries. There was no privacy at all. I could see the monitors that assessed their vital signs. Every time one sounded its alarm, I was reminded of Samuel. I hated those noises and being around all of the ailing children. Some of them slept, others moaned, and a few were coherent and talked to their families. Seeing Kate asleep and unable to wake up from the anesthesia made me uneasy, even though the surgery had apparently been successful. She breathed deeply and looked so angelic. I talked to her and stroked her long brown hair, but I got no reaction.

Cedric and I took turns staying with her. He was unable to evoke any type of response, either. I went to her again, but she was still out. I told myself that when she woke up, I would never make her stop talking again. All I wanted to hear was her sweet voice jabbering away. None of my desperate attempts roused her.

Finally, I said to my sleeping babe, "When we get back to the room, we are going to watch *Lilo & Stitch*"—her favorite movie.

Suddenly, her eyes popped open, and she looked at me. I smiled as some of my panic melted away. She was unable to say much, because the tube they had inserted in her throat during surgery irritated it. I didn't care. I was just happy to see her eyes open and shining brighter than before.

She was soon carted back to her regular room, dazed and confused, but she was there, and she was healthy. She remained complication-free and was released a day later. The events during those forty-eight hours could have been very different. Had we never met Kourtney, Kate may have faced the same demise as Jace. God used him to help us. Although Jace was only two years old when he died, he served exactly how God wanted him to, just as our Samuel did. Jace brought joy and love to his family, and his illness was a testament to us, which ultimately saved our daughter.

twenty one

The Manic Pregnancy

We brought Kate home from the hospital one day before school started. I thought that maybe, just maybe,
things would be normal for a while. I anticipated that
teaching would keep my mind occupied on something
other than the summer's dramatic events. Contact with
Kourtney was hit or miss. Some days we sent dozens of
texts and called back and forth. On other days I didn't
hear a thing. I wasn't sure which I liked better: constant updates or no news at all. I just had to assume
no news was good news, but really, on days without any
contact, I worried that she was having a rough day and
grieving.

We scheduled an appointment with the same perinatologist who had been my doctor. I had been wrong when
I thought I would never see him again. Because Kourtney
was pregnant with multiples and having issues with blood
pressure, seeing a specialist was necessary. I was excited that
Kourtney would be treated by him, because he was the best.
In the meantime, though, her general physician prescribed
her anxiety medication. Kourtney had not taken any since

the surrogacy process had begun, so I was a bit troubled about her beginning the medication while pregnant. I was very concerned about my babies and wasn't about to let anyone harm them with drugs.

"Are you sure it's safe? I'm not comfortable with you taking medication without the perinatologist's consent."

"My doctor said it's okay to take it when pregnant," she said.

"Can you wait until we see the specialist? I'd really like to get his approval before you take any anxiety medicines."

"I need something," she said, annoyed with my request. "I am going crazy. I can't sleep. I don't want to get out of bed. What am I supposed to do?"

"Let's wait until Friday. It's only three days."

"Fine. Whatever."

She was obviously grieving, and I understood the sorrow she was going through. Losing a child is the most painful life experience possible for a mother—or a father, for that matter. It's as if your identity has been stolen. You retain the title "Mother" or "Father," but your purpose in life is different. Your dreams are different. Your life revolves around "if only" and "what if." You cling to the memories, hoping they never fade. Yet with time, they do anyway. You wish the pain would fade instead, but it doesn't. Clearly, Kourtney's loss affected her more deeply than it did me. She was Jace's mother; I was not. But I had been in her shoes, and I had grieved harder and longer than anyone else when my son died. I worked through it and got myself to a functional level. Kourtney was caught somewhere between the initial shock and acceptance. I knew grieving was a long process, but I feared that our not moving forward together would put distance in our relationship.

I made several attempts to contact her and coordinate a time to pick her up for the appointment. She didn't respond until late the evening before. I hated procrastination, so her untimely reply irritated me.

PICK ME UP AT ELEVEN O'CLOCK TOMORROW, she texted.

I replied: OKAY. SEE YA THEN.

I almost sent a sarcastic text thanking her for the advance notice. It was difficult not being able to communicate my frustration with her, but I withheld it to preserve the harmony. She was grieving and deserved to be handled with gentleness. I didn't want to cause her emotional distress that might compromise the health of the babies, and I didn't want to seem like an ungrateful ass.

The next morning we headed to the perinatologist. It was a long two-hour trip, but I felt reassured to be at a specialist's office. He remembered me, probably because I was such a tough case.

"What are you here for? Are you pregnant?"

"Nope. She is—with my babies."

He gave me a funny look.

"She is my surrogate," I said.

"Oh, wow! That's awesome. I was definitely surprised to see you here. Last I remembered, you said no more pregnancies. A surrogate pregnancy. This is crazy!"

"Yep. It's twins."

His jaw dropped. "Seriously! Twins? Congratulations! Well, let's get started so we can see those babies. I need to ask Kourtney some questions first. How many pregnancies have you had?"

"Three," she said. "Two live births, one miscarriage. One of my kids just died."

The doctor's eyes widened. "Oh, my. I'm so sorry. How old?"

"He was two."

"What happened, if you don't mind my asking?"

"It was Meckel's diverticulum. It's congenital. His intestines tore, and he went septic."

"Geez. I'm sorry to hear that." There was always an awkward pause when you told someone about such a loss. "Uh . . . geez . . . um . . . did you happen to have issues with your other pregnancies? Like preterm labor or anything?" he finally asked.

"I was told I had gestational diabetes and that my blood pressure was high at the end of one pregnancy."

He cocked his head and scribbled everything down. "Are you having problems now?"

"My blood pressure has been high, and I have spotted some," Kourtney said. "I'm taking medicine for the blood pressure, and it has been better."

"Really? It's early for blood pressure to be high, unless you had a chronic condition beforehand. After losing your son, I can see where it might be a problem for you. Let's take a peek at the babies."

We watched on the big screen as he scanned her abdomen. He started to chuckle.

"What?" Kourtney asked.

"It's just crazy. Everything you just told me is crazy. You have had gestational diabetes, you have high blood pressure and have spotted with this pregnancy, and your son just died." He looked at me. "And I know you have been through the wringer! How are either of you sane?"

Kourtney shot him a go-to-hell look and pursed her lips as if to prevent a vulgarity from exiting her mouth.

God help him. He just pissed off the wrong momma.

"On the bright side of things," he said, "the babies look great. If I had to guess their genders, I'd say two girls. It's only thirteen weeks' gestation, so my guess isn't that accurate."

"I have a question," said Kourtney. "Can I take the Prozac my doctor prescribed for anxiety?"

"Yeah. It's safe," he said.

She heaved a sigh of relief.

"The only concern we have is that it might cause withdrawal effects when the babies are born. They could be more fussy or irritated, but there is not much evidence out there supporting that. There are no physical effects that have been brought to my attention. Long story short, yes, you can take it. My advice is to wean yourself off it when it's closer to the due date."

I was okay with that, hoping the medicine would relax her, so that she could start to function normally. I knew Kourtney certainly was thankful.

"How did you like him?" I asked as we left the office.

"He was okay. I didn't appreciate him laughing."

"I could tell. He is the best, so just ignore that. He really is caring. Besides that, I want you here. You and the babies will be taken care of."

I called the day a win. Kourtney kind of liked the doctor, she got permission to take medicine for her anxiety, and the babies were healthy. The encouraging days seemed few and far between. For every good day, we had about twenty or more horrendous ones. Thanks to our depressing and anxiety-filled histories, the bad days seemed a hundred times more dramatic and terrifying. When people have been persistently bombarded with negative news, they just expect the worst.

On September 5, 2011, about a week after our appointment, we had one of those unpleasant days. We were at the fourteen-week point in the pregnancy. Usually, that meant the risk of miscarriage was low. It was a point in pregnancy when expecting parents could relax just a bit. None of that normal stuff happened for us, though. We got the privilege of traveling the most complicated route.

Kourtney called me with grim news. "I woke up this morning in a pool of blood."

How could this be? It is the same thing that happened to me during my pregnancies.

"Call the perinatologist. We're going to see him," I said without a second thought. I hung up the phone.

The rage built in me, and I screamed at God, "Why do you tell us to ask for anything and it will be given to us? I feel like you are punishing me for being part of the surrogacy! I sought your will! You know I did! The puzzle fit together. Has my focus been in the wrong place? Have I been idolizing babies instead of seeking you? I thought I had grown closer to you, but now I wonder. What am I missing? Please make it clear."

I called my most trustworthy confidante, Diane, and told her to pray. Perhaps if she prayed, God would answer. He surely didn't answer me. I just wanted consistent normalcy, but I got consistent chaos. I frantically drove to the hospital and anticipated the worst when I arrived. Instead, I was met with all-too-familiar but empty and meaningless words: "The babies are good for now."

It was uncanny how Kourtney's pregnancy mimicked mine. I wanted to crawl into a hole and die, because it was too painful a reminder of all I had lost. I was sorry that Kourtney would have to experience what I did. I remembered our conversation from a year earlier. She had asked me if the problems I had were due to bad embryos. I felt like a liar. I wasn't nearly as convinced now as I had been about the health of my embryos.

Every day I waited for my spirit to be crushed under the weight of hearing that Kourtney had miscarried the babies. Every day I waited for my hope to be snatched away. My Sunday school lesson that week made it evident that to hope for things on earth was akin to chasing the wind. Hope for temporary, earthly tangibles, such as babies, could never quench the insatiable thirst I had for wholeness. I was mortal, and my time in the world was only a sliver, compared to the eternal life spent in heaven with

Jesus. The only real, lasting hope was eternity with Christ. Only he could make me whole.

Hope for that should have been enough to bring joy to my most sorrowful or anxious moments, but it wasn't. I resisted letting God have complete control over my life. The journey I had been on was riddled with fear. The unknown, hypochondria, and death were ghosts of the past that maintained their domination over my present. I considered them to be part of me, and I hated them. That was the irony of my battle. I needed to give my broken self (including the parts I despised the most) over to God so that he could burden himself, and I could be freed of the chains holding me down.

twenty two

Communication

I waited impatiently for our follow-up appointment with the doctor. I texted Kourtney nonstop during that entire week to check on her bleeding. HOW IS IT TODAY? BETTER? WORSE? HOW MUCH? WHAT COLOR?

I was obsessed with knowing.

IT'S NOT AS BAD, she'd reply, reassuring me each time.

At the appointment, the gender of the babies was revealed: one boy and one girl. Both were healthy. Kourtney's bleeding had been reduced to a scanty brown discharge. It was better than the red stuff, but I remained skeptical. I let a tiny part of me get excited and begin to consider names. Kourtney tried to convince me to start shopping, but I didn't want to jinx anything. I thought that if I got too happy, God would make something bad happen, so that it would even out the joy of the occasion. If he saw me sad all of the time, then he might spare me from any more hardships. He would feel sorry for me—maybe. Regardless, the momentary happiness gave me enough courage to career around the next blind corner.

Kourtney and I didn't talk much for the next few weeks. I figured that the lull freed her from feeling burdened to give me a play-by-play of the pregnancy while she grieved. Her mental health was just as important as her physical health. As far as pregnancy goes, the physical factors, such as ligament pain, sleep disturbances, heartburn, and simply getting fat are psychologically tasking for any woman, let alone one whose child recently died. I didn't mind the hiatus so much, either, because when we did communicate she often reemphasized how miserable she was. She didn't realize how badly I wished I could be pregnant with my own babies. I wanted to have the expanding waistline and the stretch marks. I felt annoyed that she didn't seem to consider my sensitivity to the situation. It pained me to hear negative comments about the pregnancy. I felt as if my children were a burden to her. Pregnancy would only get more cumbersome for her, which meant the grumbling would likely get worse. Despite my empathy for her, I could feel myself getting testier.

It was mid-October, and at nineteen weeks' gestation, we went to the perinatologist for the biophysical profile scan. The doctor carefully looked at each and every inch of the babies, as well as the placentas and Kourtney's womb. Everything was perfect. He saw no anomalies with the babies, Kourtney wasn't bleeding, and there were no signs of any impending crisis. We discussed delivery methods for the first time. Kourtney had her heart set on delivering vaginally, but he did only C-sections for high-risk patients.

Because the pregnancy had already had some hiccups, we were in the high-risk category.

"You are welcome to find another doctor," he said, "but it might be difficult since you are nearly halfway through the pregnancy. I'd still like to see you, even if you find someone else."

I wasn't comfortable switching doctors, because we had the best. I couldn't tell Kourtney what to do with her body, though. I didn't know what sane doctor would take a patient with such a tainted pregnancy. It was only a minor dilemma, because I had tons of experiences with several other regular OBs who possibly would meet Kourtney's approval. They were very good about communicating with the perinatologist. I was confident we would find the right doctor. It was a small inconvenience, compared to the positive news we had received during the scan. God had answered a prayer. I finally had a normal day—no drama, no fuss. However, it lasted only a few hours.

That night Kourtney called and told me her feet and ankles were swollen. That wasn't unusual in the late stages of pregnancy, but we were only halfway done. Due to the fact that she struggled to maintain normal blood pressure, I assumed that her swollen feet were a symptom of that. Her blood pressure had been under control with medication. If the issue was pregnancy-induced hypertension (PIH), medication wouldn't help. The possibility of PIH scared me. It typically resulted in early deliveries, regardless of the babies' gestational age, in order to preserve the mother's health. My babies were too young to survive outside the womb. The only telltale sign of the disease was the presence of protein in urine. So far, Kourtney was protein-free. *God, it's impossible to be hopeful. I'm waiting for the rug to be pulled out from under me again. I really want this to work.*

I honestly felt as if God owed me the babies. He owed me a good experience, which is why I was often frustrated, confused, and ultra-sensitive to any little abnormality in the pregnancy. I just could not understand how a loving God of mercy and grace could allow hurtful things to happen to his followers. *I don't want to be heartbroken again. Keep all complications away. You have the power. I do love you. Have I not suffered enough? You know what it is like to lose a child. Please spare us.*

I wish I could have said that every day my prayers were answered exactly how I wanted them to be. It would have been a lot easier to be a Christian and to convince other people that Christianity was the way to go. Who wouldn't want all of their wishes granted? But God wasn't a mythical genie. He met needs, not wants. He desired to be loved the same way I wanted to be loved: freely. There could be no price tags, no incentives, and no disclaimers.

It didn't matter how much I cried to God; things spiraled out of control. The pregnancy continued into a steady decline.

MY BLOOD PRESSURE IS HIGH, Kourtney texted.

With a heavy heart, I called and quizzed her. "How high?"

"It's been in the 150s over 90s."

Those numbers scared me. They were reminiscent of my struggle with blood pressure after my first miscarriage.

"Did you call the doctor?" I asked.

"No!" she yelled. "I am just stressed out right now! I want to talk about Jace, and Nathan doesn't. He just goes out to hunt raccoons all the time. I'm here alone every night, and I hate it!"

I sensed that the waxing and waning of her blood pressure were due to stress in her house and not the pregnancy, although the latter got the blame. I had wondered about stress even before Jace died. Neither she nor the babies needed the added anxiety. I was tired of the drama. I had my own issues. I didn't want to be involved in her personal life outside of the pregnancy, and I sure didn't want the babies to suffer because of it.

I broke down and wailed on the phone, "I don't know what to do! This just isn't working. Everything that could possibly go wrong has! Just go to the hospital, I guess."

Her tone completely changed. "No, I don't want to do that. I'll just lie down and rest. I can take another pill if I want. I'm just not sure how much longer I'm going to last."

I was confused. She went from rage to serenity when I mentioned the hospital. When she got stressed, I reacted by freaking out. But once I freaked out, then she got calm. It seemed so antagonistic, which wasn't going to work in a surrogate pregnancy where everyone needed to function as one for the sake of the babies. Either she really didn't understand how emotional a time it was for me, because she was consumed with her own loss, or she was intentionally pushing my buttons to get me riled up so that I would give her attention. I felt exhausted from trying to solve problems for both of us. I had constant nausea, heartburn, and sleepless nights. I thought I would be driven to lunacy if God didn't stop the endless roller-coaster. I doubted myself. I doubted Kourtney. I doubted God. The cycle repeated itself.

Why, God? Why have you chosen me? I'm inadequate. I'm ill-equipped for this task. My weaknesses are being exposed. Renew me. Bring joy. Bring the babies safely to us. My prayers were followed up with sighs. I was drained.

Kourtney had another appointment right around Halloween. Full of horrors of every kind, it was par for the course with us. Her blood pressure registered at 160/90. The doctor was much less concerned with that once Kourtney revealed she had been having contractions.

It was the first I had heard about it. I shook my head in disgust as she explained that some of them were intense and happening frequently. I was less shocked and more angry at her for not telling me when they had first started. I just assumed that since she was including me in the rest of her drama, I would have heard about that as well. Contractions at twenty-two weeks were sort of worth mentioning. I felt betrayed. How could I put any more trust in her to do the right thing with my kids? *God? Where are you? Help would be good right about now.*

twenty three

Sustainability

At the beginning of November, we had our very first appointment with a doctor who was willing to take Kourtney and deliver her vaginally. He had been my regular OB with Samuel. I was very confident in his abilities and judgment. His bedside manner was superior to most, and he seemed to care about his patients. He was never afraid to offer a prayer or another similar gesture. He measured up to Kourtney's standards, and she was instantly in love with him. As an added bonus, his office was much closer to our homes. We still met with the perinatologist; therefore, appointments were staggered about every two weeks. That was a good thing, due to the ever-present blood pressure fluctuations and contractions to boot.

Once the pregnancy reached twenty-four weeks, we finally had a bit of breathing room. It was a point where the babies could be born and could live outside the womb, but they would require a lot of intervention to survive. Still, it was a major triumph, despite everything that had gone wrong. Our next checkup revealed a new problem: Kourtney's cervix was shortening. The normal length of a cervix at that point of gestation was 4 cm. Her cervix was about 1.5 cm. The change was due to the bustling babies applying lots of pressure. Statistics showed that Kourtney had a 50 percent chance of going into preterm labor.

"It's best for you to go on bed rest," the doctor told her. "I'm also giving you a shot that can help postpone labor. Neither bed rest nor the shot are guarantees, though."

Kourtney let out a sigh that transformed into an annoyed growl. "Am I going to be able to attend family gatherings? The holidays are coming up soon, and the funeral home is hosting an ornament ceremony honoring the deceased. I was going to attend for my son."

"You can do some stuff, but you really need to be off your feet as much as possible. You and Kenzie should probably discuss what is acceptable."

I did not appreciate his throwing that decision into my lap. I knew that bed rest was awful, especially around the holidays. A person might as well be locked in a tiny cell with no windows or door. Idleness was a psychological killer to an active person. You can only occupy your mind so long by staring at a computer, a television, or a book. You feel trapped, and it eventually drives you to the point of insanity.

What made the situation even worse was that Kourtney was going on bed rest, rather than me. I knew I was capable of suffering through it, but she wasn't me. She was in a vulnerable place, having already lost part of her family. I wondered whether she had the mental strength to do it.

I wouldn't be around to baby-sit her and ensure that she followed the doctor's orders. My trust in her had already faltered. God was the only one able to be on patrol 24/7. *Nothing can be easy, can it God? I can't control what she does outside of my presence. Please take care of the babies, regardless of her choices.*

I had a difficult choice to make. I could deny her the opportunity to celebrate what would already be a depressing holiday season without her son, or I could really let God handle the details. At that point, I had not been able to change his mind about the direction the pregnancy had gone.

"I would rather you lie in bed all the time with your butt propped up on pillows, pointed to the sky. I did that, but it didn't change the outcome. My baby still died. I would be okay with you going to gatherings as long as you are off your feet. You have help during the day. I'll come over in the evenings after work to clean and fix meals, so you can rest."

"Well, I guess that could work. Nate can handle Lilly, but he would need help cooking and cleaning. Are you sure you want to do this?"

"It's not a problem. I want to help you. It's the least I can do." My babies had reached a point of viability, so I was willing to do anything to reduce the load Kourtney bore.

I thought that volunteering my services would be an easy fix to the stress. I had no idea how tired I would be. Thanksgiving week was not the best time to start a second job. I worked from 8 a.m. to 4 p.m. at school, then went straight to Kourtney's until 9 p.m. to pick up, wash, scrub, and cook.

I wasn't opposed to cleanliness. I was a neat person, but cleaning for an individual who proclaimed that she was obsessive was like trying to satisfy a smoker with candy cigarettes. Kourtney had particular cleaning methods, and they were not the same as mine. It didn't bother me to use a regular toilet brush to clean the toilets. She wanted hers scrubbed with a purple toothbrush that had soft bristles, using a clockwise motion for three minutes. I didn't know whether I was helping or making things worse. I felt exhausted and didn't care about her opinion of my cleaning techniques. I wasn't necessarily doing it for her anyway. The health and well-being of my babies were my main motivations for helping.

Cooking for her and her family was an even bigger pain than cleaning. They were more of a meat and taters family. My family ate salad—rabbit food. She cooked with fat. I cooked with fat-free cooking spray. Fat certainly made everything taste better, but I was obsessive when it came to fats in my food. I limited them a great deal. In other words, almost everything I cooked was gross. I should have taken the hint when Kourtney and her family never seemed very hungry on the evenings when I made their meals.

Working with students seven hours every day at school was easy compared to the laborious evenings at Kourtney's. I felt tired just thinking about it. Playing the maidservant role was not in my usual repertoire, but it allowed me to develop a greater appreciation for caretakers and the time they sacrifice for their loved ones. Cedric and my siblings had done that for me. Their demonstration of selfless love was a legacy for me to carry on. I wasn't able to care for and nurture my babies directly, but I could indirectly by doing my best to serve the woman who carried them in her womb.

We remained in a state of flux at the twenty-six-week checkup. I prayed for sunshine but got rain. Kourtney's cervical length had shortened to 0.9 cm. The perinatologist wanted her on strict bed rest. She shouldn't get up, except to use the bathroom. The chance of that happening was nil. She had not yet gone to the ceremony that honored Jace, and she hadn't had Christmas with her extended family. Because her cervix had been dramatically reduced to nearly half the length it had been two weeks prior, I was suspicious whether she was resting at all. I would never be able to know. I wished I could have set up a hidden camera so that I wouldn't have to make assumptions. I despised the unknown.

One benefit of going to this appointment was steroid shots, which the doctor gave Kourtney to strengthen the babies' lungs. I had received them with Samuel; however, I had no fluid in the amniotic sac. That had prevented his lungs from maturing. The twins' sacs were perfect. On an ultrasound, the doctor had pointed out that the babies were exercising their lungs with the fluid. Steroid shots would be very beneficial, because it seemed as if an early delivery was imminent. Kourtney received a series of the shots over a forty-eight-hour period.

The very next day, she texted me to say that she'd had lots of contractions the previous evening. She'd had so many that she and Nathan were in the car ready to go to the hospital, but the contractions suddenly stopped. It was a little disturbing, because she had let them go on for hours and hadn't called me or the doctors. The babies could have been born alive at twenty-six weeks; however, they would require a lot of care at a hospital in a neonatal intensive care unit (NICU). The nearest one was more than two hours from Kourtney. Waiting around to see what happened could have been a life-or-death choice for my children. Because of Jace's quick and unexpected passing, I thought she would have erred on the side of caution when it came to the babies. I had zero tolerance for carelessness. If something happened to my babies because she lacked due diligence, I would be enraged.

ʒʘ

At every consecutive appointment, the situation remained tenuous. Each one, though, meant we were one step closer to having healthy babies. They hung in there, seemingly unaffected by the dramatic changes that affected Kourtney. By mid-December, her cervix was barely visible at 0.4 cm. The twins each weighed more than three pounds at twenty-eight weeks' gestation. Many times, it felt as if we were sliding backward, but we slowly conquered each milestone.

Back in September, when Kourtney had the major bleeding episode, I had prayed that the pregnancy would last to thirty weeks. On Christmas Day 2011, God answered that prayer. I had doubted the entire time, but God proved me wrong again. The doctors were amazed that Kourtney's uterus had held up for so long, albeit not perfectly. Each day after thirty weeks seemed like a bonus.

The rest of Kourtney wasn't fairing so well, though. I received a constant barrage of negative texts from her, each one uniquely describing her disdain for the situation. She shouldn't have expected anything but misery at that point in the pregnancy, but I knew her misery was more than just physical. It was her first Christmas without Jace. I had no doubt she suffered from a broken heart.

Both the OB and the perinatologist started doing non-stress tests (NSTs) on Kourtney twice a week. NSTs were performed to record the babies' movements and heart rates. The infants continued to grow (more than four pounds each) and were performing well.

Then we received some discouraging news during one of the NSTs. Kourtney was contracting quite a bit more than the doctor was comfortable with, and follow-up ultrasounds revealed that her cervix was dilated. He admitted her to the hospital on New Year's Eve, and she would have to stay at least one night for more monitoring. Needless to say, she was not excited about celebrating the New Year in the hospital, but it was not as if she had a party to attend.

I, conversely, felt happy because she was in the facility with the best NICU in the state, just in case we needed it that night. I didn't know how things would turn out, so I stayed around quite a while until Nathan arrived and the contractions subsided. I celebrated the arrival of 2012 during my drive home, lost in thought, hoping it was a less theatrical year than the previous one.

twenty four

The Last Straw

It was obvious that the pregnancy was becoming more unstable. Our local hospital didn't have a NICU and wouldn't
deliver women under thirty-four weeks' gestation. We had
almost four more weeks until the pregnancy met that cri-
teria. If Kourtney was discharged, she would go home. I
wanted her to stay near the hospital with the NICU. Her
home was two hours away; however, she had family who
lived within a few minutes of the medical facility.

My initial inclination was to ask her to stay with family
members who could provide housing, help with meal preparation, and keep a watchful eye on her. It would certainly
be more economical for us, because our funds were being
depleted very quickly. I was more than willing to pay some
sort of rent. Several hundred dollars' rent for one month
was much cheaper than $100 a night for a hotel room and
fast food. It also got me off the hook from working for her
in the evenings. It was a masterful plan, if Kourtney would
come on board. More likely than not, I would have to make
a decision she wouldn't agree with.

"I really would like you to stay near the NICU," I said. "It's just safer at this point."

"What is Nathan supposed to do? He has to work. He can't stay down here with me. And what do I do with Lilly?"

"If you stayed with family in the area, I don't think Nathan and Lilly would need to stay every day. They could go home. He can work, and Lilly can still go to preschool. I'd pay for any extra daycare she might need."

Kourtney sat stoically in bed without uttering a word. The sour look on her face told me it was going to take much convincing to get her to agree with my plan.

"I stayed with relatives when I was on bed rest and Cedric worked. My family cared for Kate when I couldn't. It's only a maximum of four weeks. Then our local hospital can care for you and the babies."

As expected, my idea was not well received. She immediately started in with excuses.

"Who will take me to my twice-a-week appointments?"

"I can take you on Tuesdays," I responded enthusiastically. "Nathan can take you on Fridays, since he doesn't work that day."

"I'm not sure my family will have room for me. My cousin's house is small, and my sister-in-law has a spare bed, but it gets used sometimes."

I didn't voice the sarcastic comment that popped into my head.

"Plus, my sister-in-law has animals in the house. We are allergic to indoor pets."

Her ability to nitpick every suggestion to death was mind-numbing. Instead of reacting forcefully, though, I tried a different approach, one that might provoke compassion, rather than animosity.

"This is important to the health of the babies. What if you go into labor at home? You are two hours from a NICU suitable enough to care for preemies. The babies won't do well in a two-hour car ride if born at thirty or so weeks' gestation."

She countered with this comment: "We could call the medical helicopter. They service our area. Our yard is big enough to land on."

I tilted my head from side to side, cracking the tensed vertebrae that seemed bound by the absurdity of her idea. Was she serious? She was going to summon a helicopter to pick her up and carry her off to the NICU. She grasped for any straw she could get her hands on. My kids' lives depended on her to make the best decision for them. Personal discomfort impeded her ability to make good choices, so I pressed harder.

"I think it would be best to stay with family for a while until the babies could be delivered safely at our local hospital. I know it's inconvenient, but I'm not willing to risk you being two hours away from the NICU at this stage of the pregnancy."

She was not unaware of the facts; she knew the pregnancy was at a critical point. Everything had changed for the worse. The only stabilizing factor in the situation was being close to a NICU, where appropriate treatment could be given if the babies came too early.

Kourtney contacted her cousin. As I'd expected, she didn't have to convince anyone to let her stay with them. She was very pregnant with someone else's kids, and she had lost her own son only months earlier. Anyone with half a heart wouldn't turn away a woman in that situation.

Kourtney was discharged late on New Year's Day. Within hours, she was moved into her cousin's home. The house was small but big enough to accommodate one extra person. It would be a much tighter fit with Nathan and Lilly tagging along on the weekends, though. As a gesture of goodwill, I loaned Kourtney my laptop. I hoped it would deflect some of the resentment she may have felt after I strongly encouraged her stay in a foreign place. In addition to that, I figured that sitting idle would not be helpful to her psyche. Downtime often spawned trouble, such as anxiety and depression. The scenario at her cousin's seemed perfect. Yet it was too perfect. Nothing about the surrogacy had been perfect. That should have set off alarm bells.

Kourtney called me with another excuse only a few days after being at her cousin's. "The house is just not big enough, and her ex-roommate is probably moving back. It will be easier for me to relax at home. *And* I'm pretty sure I broke your laptop. I tripped on the cord, and it fell off the table. We'll buy you a new one sometime."

I felt annoyed that she'd mentioned wanting to go home *again.* As for the broken laptop, how could I ever demand they buy a new one, since she was helping us out in a big way by carrying our babies? I gritted my teeth. "Don't worry about it. Just take care of the babies. That is the most important thing right now." I hoped that forgiving her debt would persuade her to stick with the plan of staying near the NICU.

"Is there someone else you could stay with?" I asked. "You mentioned a sister-in-law once."

I knew I was pushing my luck. It was asking a lot of her and her family, but for the sake of my babies I was willing to exhaust every resource she or I had.

"I can ask her," she said, aggravated at my persistence.

"That would be really helpful," I said.

Several days later, Kourtney moved to her sister-in-law's house. During all of the shuffling around, we checked in with the perinatologist. Kourtney was dilated 4 cm and 90 percent effaced. In other words, her cervix was open and stretching with all of the pressure the babies put on it. At thirty-two weeks, they each weighed more than five pounds; they were nice and plump for their age and showing no signs of distress.

The relationship between Kourtney and me was a different story. She insisted on going home, but I asserted that she and the babies would be better off staying close to the hospital for two more weeks.

"You're almost done," I assured her, over and over.

She repeatedly voiced her unhappiness with her living arrangements. I ignored it until the day she rushed Lilly to the emergency room because of a mild allergic reaction she had to the cat residing in her sister-in-law's home.

"I am not staying here anymore," Kourtney said. "Lilly's allergies are acting up. She can't breathe here."

I was dumbfounded as to why she insisted on having her family constantly at her side anyway. A few nights away from her husband and daughter weren't going to kill her. I had spent countless days and nights alone, because of my husband's job as a pilot. I was simply calloused to it. I wanted Kourtney to give adequate time and attention to my children in her womb, because the status of the pregnancy was at a critical stage. Since four-year-olds are very demanding, I worried that Lilly might shift Kourtney's focus away from the pregnancy. However, I certainly was not about to ask that she cease having any contact with her only child. I attempted to make another concession.

"You have less than two weeks left to reach thirty-four. I'm not comfortable with you going home yet. We can try to get an extended stay hotel for you." I groveled until she agreed, but she remained malcontent.

I did everything I could to locate a hotel somewhat near the hospital. I was looking for homey and economical. Those specific conditions made it all the more difficult. I located one on the Internet that seemed decent. It didn't appear to have luxurious accommodations, but the reviews didn't indicate that it was crawling with roaches and bed bugs, either. It had the amenities Kourtney and her family would need to cook meals and be able to spread out and relax a little bit. I mentioned the prospective hotel to Kourtney, and she went bananas.

"My mother-in-law said that place stinks. She stayed there a long time ago, and it was nasty. I'm not staying there."

I was at my wit's end. Kourtney had formed her opinion before she even explored the option on the table. Our surrogacy contract had never stated luxury hotels; lodging had to be reasonable. I realized that her reasonable and my reasonable were not the same. As long as the hotel room wasn't infested with bugs or smoked in or didn't have bed sheets covered in hair, I was good to go. I didn't want to get ugly and be all business with her, but I had no choice. We were so close to seeing the pregnancy through to a safe point.

I raised my voice, "You don't even know," but I bit my tongue before something worse came out. "You haven't stayed there. If it's that bad, we can do something else, but going home is not an option right now."

She was thirty-three weeks' pregnant, uncomfortable, depressed, and just wanted to be home. I understood her plight and empathized, but I was ready to wash my hands of her. Her negativity and dissatisfaction with everything fatigued me. My objectives were for the babies to be safely born and for Kourtney and me to go our separate ways. These objectives couldn't be achieved soon enough.

Two days after she checked into the hotel, the proverbial poo hit the fan. Kourtney voiced her objection about the accommodations. It smelled. The neighbors were loud. It was too dirty. Nothing about it was acceptable. She was determined to be disgruntled. I was done. I lit into her with an essay-long text message. Of course, written communication had a tendency to lose its luster, so my angry texting didn't effectively convey how I really felt.

IF I COULD HAVE CARRIED MY OWN CHILDREN, I WOULD HAVE! BUT GUESS WHAT, IT DIDN'T WORK OUT THAT WAY. I KNOW THIS A BURDEN TO YOU AND YOUR FAMILY, BUT NO ONE MADE YOU DO THIS. NO ONE FORCED THIS UPON YOU, SO DON'T GET PISSY! WE HAVE DONE EVERYTHING WE CAN TO HELP. I HAVE SPENT WEEKS AWAY FROM HOME, LIVING IN HOSPITALS AND OTHER PEOPLE'S HOUSES. YOU NAME IT, I'VE DONE IT. AND I STILL LOST THREE BABIES. I GOT NOTHING. YOU WERE THE ANGEL THAT GAVE US THIS CHANCE, SO PLEASE DON'T GET UPSET BECAUSE WE CAN'T AFFORD A FIVE-STAR HOTEL.

I was tired of her insolence. She rejected every kind gesture we made to her. I called Cedric to vent. He was just leaving the airport and happened to be in the area of the hotel.

"I hate her! She is griping about the hotel now! It is supposedly smelly and loud. Go over there and see if what she is telling me is true."

He went to investigate and to try to smooth things over with—*sandwiches?* He was such a clever man. Attempting to appease a pregnant lady with food was genius. He was always good at damage control. He reported back that there were no issues with the hotel room.

I couldn't believe that she had misled me. And for what? A fancier hotel? A pardon to release her to her home? We had been faithful about taking care of all surrogacy expenses, and she had treated us like doormats. I was at my breaking point, and I lost all sympathy for her. She had willingly put herself out there, knowing unforeseen events could happen. In our case, they occurred with a vengeance, and she had not handled it with the maternal maturity I'd hoped for. Obviously, our five-year age difference and my experience with bad pregnancies far surpassed her understanding and ability to cope with how reality often presented itself.

The next day after our spat, Kourtney made the choice to go back home. I couldn't stop her. She was nearly thirty-four weeks' pregnant, and every single day was important. The helpless feelings I had experienced during my first miscarriage reemerged. God continued to exercise his sovereignty over the situation I wanted to control.

twenty five
Baby Shower

January 25, two days after returning home, Kourtney went to the local hospital with contractions. Our regular OB determined that her cervix was dilated 8 cm. Even though she wasn't in active labor, he told her she had to stay in the hospital until the babies decided to make their appearance. The doctor planned to give her another round of steroid shots, because he anticipated delivering the babies within the week. I got a warm fuzzy feeling, knowing she wasn't going anywhere. She would be a resident until she gave birth. Inside, I was gloating.

Yet everything was happening too fast. Reality sank in that I was probably going to be a new mother very soon. I had looked forward to the day but suddenly didn't feel ready. It was difficult to make the mental transition from manager to mother.

Watching and coaching from the sidelines as someone else carried your baby was so much different than being pregnant for nearly a year and feeling a baby grow inside of you. You miss out on the experience of feeling the baby kick in response to your voice or music; you can't feel it squirm when you lie in a position it doesn't like; and you don't get to feel the baby hiccup for hours at a time after you drink a soda or eat a candy bar. In an instant, you go from having no baby to one lying nestled in your arms. I was afraid I wouldn't feel connected to the babies or they wouldn't feel connected to me. Maybe they would be distressed at not being near Kourtney once they were born. I wondered if, in the future, they would feel more bonded to her than to me when they saw her. Worse yet, what if she bonded with them and wanted to keep them? I worked myself into a frenzy with all of the scenarios. The fact was, I had taken a leap of faith and waited . . . and waited . . . and waited some more for God to reveal his will.

In addition to failing at the mental preparation, I failed at the physical as well. I hadn't purchased a single item, set up the nursery, or anything. It was the way I protected myself. If the babies died, I didn't want to have baby items sitting around, reminding me of what could have been. Their chances of survival were good, but we wouldn't know what setbacks they might have with their lungs or feeding abilities until birth. At thirty-four to thirty-five weeks, it could go either way, according to our doctor.

For several days the medical staff scurried around, monitoring and assessing Kourtney and the babies. The nurses administered magnesium to stop the contractions and to prevent full-blown labor for at least a few more days. The drugs to stop labor were no picnic. Kourtney looked dreadful. Every inch of her body was swollen with fluid. Her bright blue eyes were squished and smothered by her puffy face. Her hands looked as if they had been replaced with inflated rubber gloves. Often she had a damp wash-cloth covering her forehead to ease the headaches caused by the medicine. Another day passed, and then another. Each day Kourtney looked a little more exhausted.

The day marking thirty-four weeks' gestation came and went. It seemed as if she was in a steady holding pattern, 8 cm dilated and contracting occasionally. I stuck around before and after work as much as I could to show my support and just in case something happened.

On January 30, Kourtney celebrated her birthday in the hospital. Our doctor came in early that morning to check her cervix and to monitor the babies. He must have been feeling extra nice since it was her birthday, because he sur-prised her by letting her get up and shower. He said, "Get cleaned up and ready to go. You're having babies today. Today is the day!"

"What? Seriously?" Kourtney and I clamored.

"Yep. It's really best I do it now. The steroid shots for their lungs are most effective a few days after I adminis-tered them. In other words, the babies' lungs will work bet-ter at this point than, let's say, three more days from now. It sounds backward, but the steroids sort of wear off after a certain point."

"It seems so early. Are you sure the benefits outweigh the risks?" I asked.

"There are always risks in delivery, no matter what the baby's age. I wouldn't do this if I wasn't confident in their health at this point."

"I'm ready to do this!" Kourtney exclaimed.

The babies had made it almost to thirty-five weeks' gestation. I understood his reasoning for inducing labor, but I didn't want to rush things. I was not 100 percent in favor of the doctor's choice. Kourtney was stable, sort of. She wasn't in active labor, at least. I was willing to wait it out, especially since she wasn't allowed to go anywhere, but I knew she was ready to end it. And ultimately, it *was* her body that carried the babies, so she had the final say. The babies' lungs were presumably strong enough; therefore, a safe delivery was possible. If the doctor was certain it was not dangerous, I was good to go. If anything were to happen because he was wrong, he would put his malpractice insurance to use.

I hurried back to work to get six weeks of lesson plans ready, due to my taking maternity leave. Excitement and nervousness took over; I could barely think about what I had planned to teach that day, let alone organize weeks of material. I got everything in order and met Cedric when he dropped Kate off at school. We left for the hospital; it was a short fifteen-minute drive to the end of a very long journey. With one step after another, sometimes forward and sometimes back, we endured. We were finally at the pinnacle.

჻჻

There was little for us to do at the hospital but wait and sign paperwork. The latter was chaotic. Our surrogacy was the first the hospital had ever encountered. Dealing with it from the legal vantage point was confusing. I was the biological mother, but Kourtney carried the babies. No one knew who was to be the legal guardian of the babies and who would make decisions for them, such as whether to receive vaccines right after birth. So, we both signed the documents. The hospital personnel never once mentioned that the state of Oklahoma didn't recognize Cedric or me as the biological parents of the babies. I figured no one else knew the laws. We all agreed that if it wasn't going to be challenged, we would remain mute about the subject. We hoped we could sign the paperwork for the birth certificates before the hospital or any other legal entity realized the mistake. It was underhanded, but they were our babies, not Kourtney's or Nathan's. I didn't feel obligated to explain Oklahoma laws, especially since I considered them outdated, prejudicial, bureaucratic absurdities.

We felt pretty good about things. Kourtney was given an epidural around 9:30 a.m., and the doctor broke her water at ten o'clock. She had been dilated to 8 cm all week, so she didn't have very far to go before she could start pushing to get our babies out of her and into our longing arms.

We anxiously waited. The nurses, Nathan, Cedric, and I watched Kourtney and the monitors. The contractions were getting more intense, but the babies reacted well to them. They were doing great under the stress. Another nurse came in to prepare beds and medical devices that would be used to intervene if the babies had trouble breathing. It was unsettling to see such equipment, but the nurse at the helm was my pastor's wife, the Bible study leader, and my friend. I was surprised to see Linda there; however, I was comforted by her presence. She had supported me during my journey through child loss. I knew she was there because she wanted to be, and she would do everything in her power to help our babies. I talked briefly with her. She had shifted her schedule just for us.

"I wasn't going to miss this," she said with a reassuring smile.

I imagined that a lot of people who had shared in our rough journey wanted to be there to witness God's miracles. I knew their hearts were with us, and that was enough.

Kourtney's nurse checked her cervix about 11:00 a.m. "On the next contraction, I want you to push," she said.

We were ready. Cedric and I stood upstream of Kourtney, slightly away from the bed so she could maintain a bit of privacy and dignity. We readied our cameras. Every time she pushed, I pushed with her. I grimaced, held my breath, and let it out just as Kourtney did once the contraction was over.

At twenty-five minutes after the hour, the nurse hollered, "Okay, stop pushing! Stop pushing! It's time! Page the doctor, now! Kourtney, don't push!"

"I can't help it," she growled. "I need to push!"

After a couple of minutes, the doctor literally ran in. The nurses helped him with his gown, but it was only half on before he looked down and said, "Oh, this baby is coming."

He sat on his stool just in time to catch our son. Brody Daniel was born at 11:28 a.m. Linda cleaned him up and assessed his condition. He weighed a healthy six pounds, thirteen ounces. He was crying, he was pink, and he didn't need any supplemental oxygen.

We rushed over to hold him but kept a close eye on Kourtney and our daughter, who was yet to be delivered. We gushed with happiness. We held a baby in our arms. He was really ours. We were overjoyed and humbled by God's precious gift and his choosing us to be the baby's parents. God did it. He had answered our prayers after our years of struggle and disappointment. We finally had one miracle and waited for another.

Our baby girl put up a fight. She was not coming to us so easily. She decided to turn face-up in the birth canal, instead of taking the easiest escape route, which was face-down. Kourtney pushed hard with each contraction, but our daughter was not budging, due to her head position.

The doctor was concerned about her heart rate. He attempted to place several probes on her head to monitor for heart decelerations during contractions, but they wouldn't stick. It was obvious that he worked with a purpose. He made the decision to pull her out with a vacuum. I had never witnessed the extraction of a baby with a vacuum. I didn't know there was such a procedure. I was horrified at the thought of him wheeling in a shop-vac, flipping a switch, and sucking her out with the upholstery attachment. *How in the world could vacuuming a baby be safe when they have warnings on those things saying, "Do not attach to skin or face?" Isn't a baby fragile?*

The baby vacuum turned out to be a small handheld pump that attached to the top of the baby's head. However, I still feared that it might damage my daughter's delicate body.

The doctor warned us, "Her head will probably be mis-shapen after this, but it will go back to normal. If we can't get her out this way, we will be going to the operating room for an emergency C-section."

I knew Kourtney did not want that. I just wanted my daughter out, and I didn't care how, as long as she wasn't harmed.

The doctor violently pulled and tugged on her head with the vacuum. Beads of sweat dripped off his forehead, and the veins in his forearms bulged. I thought he was going to pull her head off her body. I snuck a peek and saw her. I could see that the top of her forehead was deformed and bruised from the suction of the vacuum.

After almost thirty nail-biting minutes, our daughter's face was finally visible. With a small push from Kourtney, Laney Kai officially entered our lives at 11:57 a.m. She did not look good. Her head was in the shape of an egg-plant and just as purple. It looked terribly painful, but she was doing wonderfully as they cleaned her and checked her vitals. She weighed six pounds, two ounces. Everyone in the room was surprised at how big the twins were for being born at about thirty-five weeks' gestation. Kourtney was very lucky she didn't carry them to the normal term of forty weeks. They might have been ten pounds each!

Indeed, we had been given two healthy miracles. We didn't get to see the babies for long, however. They were taken to the nursery to get a thorough evaluation from the pediatrician. Even though they acted like full-term babies and were doing amazingly well, the medical staff wanted to keep a close watch on them for a few hours. We couldn't go into the nursery yet, so we informed our family and friends, who were waiting in the lobby, about the great news. Cheers went up as we announced the twins' safe arrival.

As we celebrated and patiently waited to see the babies again, a woman we didn't know interrupted the party. She introduced herself and said she was from records and was in charge of submitting birth certificate information to the state office of vital records. I felt uneasy and just knew she was getting ready to give us bad news. Instead, she told us something that we thought was another miracle.

"You both will be put on the birth certificates as the parents of the babies," she said, revealing her pride with a smile.

It was another cause for celebration. We could not believe how blessed we were. We'd assumed we would have a lot of legal rigamarole to deal with, in order to make the babies lawfully ours. We had been told we would have to adopt our biological children. Our attorney had been wrong all along. We weren't exactly sure where the lady from records got her information, but we weren't about to complain. We praised God.

હ્રૈજ્જી

In the middle of all the excitement over the delivery, I felt a guilty tug at my heart. While we celebrated new life and looked forward to a bright future with our growing family, Kourtney lay in a hospital bed, no longer being fussed over or coddled. She had no babies to attend to and no family or friends to visit and celebrate with her.

I was still upset over the drama she'd created and her negativity. I resented her for complaining about her misery with my children in her womb. I took those things personally, because I had done everything to make life easier for her and safe for my babies. Yet it was never good enough. I gave her the benefit of the doubt, because I was flawed myself. I had been in friendships, as well as my own marriage, where I had treated the other individual with disrespect. It was easy to do, because I knew I would be forgiven; I was still going to be loved. Many times I took things for granted or took advantage of someone, resulting in hurt feelings and sometimes resentment. Occasionally, the road to forgiveness was a long one, but I realized the importance of it, and I appreciated people who forgave me even more. Had I not been forgiven, I would have been a very lonely person.

God commanded me to forgive as well. Because he had unexpectedly brought Kourtney into our lives to perform his miracles, I would have been disregarding God's will if I completely cut her out of my life. Ungrateful wasn't what I wanted to be, nor would God or anyone else have been impressed. I didn't expect her to ask for forgiveness, because I don't think she realized how hurtful she had been. I couldn't just walk away, though, leaving behind a fellow grieving mother. There was a club—a sisterhood—that we would *always* belong to, no matter what stage of grief, the age at which our child had died, or the miles that separated us.

I went back to Kourtney's room, alone, not really knowing what I was going to say.

"How are you feeling?" I asked.

"Better. The doctor is letting me go home tonight."

"That's great. That should make you feel good."

"Yeah. Sort of."

"What do you mean? You've been wanting to go home for a long time; now you don't want to?" I said jokingly.

"I won't have anything to think about except Jace. I was occupied with your twins for so long. I don't know what to do."

I knew that lost feeling—the feeling of helplessness, the feeling of not being able to move forward, the feeling of sadness that ceaselessly grasps your soul and squeezes the will to live out of you.

I looked past her bleary eyes, right into her heart, and felt her pain. There were no words to fix it. The truth was, I still grieved the loss of Samuel. Time didn't erase my hurt, I just got used to living with it. Kourtney would have to do the same in her own time and on her own terms.

I left her room, having said very little. My mind was reeling on that day, which I thought would never happen. Thanks to Kourtney, it had. I wasn't the touchy-feely type, but I needed to show my gratitude better than I had. Even though she had been a pain in the rear, she deserved some kind words that were from my heart. Ironically, I used our broken laptop with a barely readable screen to send her a message via social media.

TO KOURTNEY, WORDS CAN'T DESCRIBE HOW HAPPY YOU HAVE MADE US. WE WILL NEVER BE ABLE TO SAY THANK YOU ENOUGH FOR YOUR SACRIFICE. WE ARE ETERNALLY GRATEFUL. I AM SURE YOUR BABY BOY IS LOOKING DOWN FROM HEAVEN SAYING, "WELL DONE, MOMMA. WELL DONE." LOVE, THE JANZENS

ॐ∞

After what seemed like an eternity of waiting, Cedric and I finally got to go into the nursery to hold the babies. Nurses were feeding them and monitoring their breathing, sucking, and swallowing reflexes.

"They are doing really well," said Linda. "They have this down perfectly. We're watching their oxygen saturation levels. They dip down just a bit when they eat, but it recovers quickly."

My head whipped toward the monitors. It rattled my nerves to hear about a decrease in oxygen saturation. We had experienced more than our fair share during Samuel's passing. I watched their levels closely.

"It's nothing alarming," she reassured me. "We're going to move them into a room with you as soon as one is available."

Cedric and I took turns being with the babies for several hours until a private room was ready. We set up camp and visited with friends and family. The babies were wheeled down in a tiny bed they both shared. It was a fight for who got to hold them first.

Kate was the exception. She wanted nothing to do with them. Every time we held one of the babies near her, she said, "Get *it* away from me!"

We had been so occupied with the health of the pregnancy that we hadn't discussed how new babies would impact the dynamics of the family. We had not prepared Kate for the baby invasion. At the time, I thought I was protecting her feelings by not building her hopes. I couldn't blame her reaction. She had been the center of our world for seven years. I regarded her as our miracle baby. Yet despite her present protests and probable future objections to sharing, we were magnificently blessed with her and her brother and sister.

twenty six

Legal Battles

Once night fell, the exhaustion set in—not just from the busy day, but also from the previous four years. Cedric and I and the twins crashed. They were cozied up to each other in their bed, sleeping peacefully, while Cedric and I lay crammed head to toe in a twin-size hospital bed. Sleeping with a man's size-thirteen feet in your face was less than intimate.

Sleep was fleeting anyway. If we weren't getting up to feed babies and change diapers, the nurses were waking us to ask questions about the children who slept comfortably next to us. It had been more than seven years since we had cared for a newborn. I likened the first child to a honeymoon period. We had been so enamored with Kate; we apparently forgot about getting puked on, peed on, pooped on, and sleep deprived. The twins made us veterans overnight.

The next day's events had to have been set in motion by Satan himself. The woman in records, who had given us the wonderful news regarding the twins' birth certificates, returned as one of the devil's minions. She didn't greet us with a smile and a chipper demeanor as she had the day before.

In a curt tone, she said, "After I spoke with state vital records and hospital attorneys, neither of you will be going on the birth certificates. You are *not* considered the parents of the babies in question."

I shouldn't have been so shocked, but I was. I wanted to bawl. I felt as if we were receiving punishment for concealing the facts about whose names should actually go on the birth certificates, according to state law.

Cedric quickly refuted her. "I will sign a paternity document that acknowledges I am the father. Our attorney told us that it is legal and will get my name on the birth certificates at least."

She fired back, "Sorry, but we won't accept that."

We were confused. The information we had received from our attorney contradicted what the woman was saying.

Cedric was fuming. "You won't accept a legally binding document created by the state of Oklahoma for this very circumstance—of who the real father is?"

"No. I told you what I was informed, and that is what I'm going with," she said. "As far as this hospital is concerned, Nathan Keeton is the father."

Hearing that made me sick. We were in a big bind.

"But wait a minute," Cedric said. "So if he denies paternity by signing a legal document, and I accept paternity by signing a legal document, you won't send my name in to the state to be put on the birth certificate?"

"That's right," she sneered.

I wanted to scratch her eyes out. Perhaps she was jaded by years of paternity scandals, but our situation was hardly scandalous. She seemed sadistic, as if she enjoyed playing the role of a witch. She had a much different attitude than she'd had twenty-four hours earlier. When we first met with our attorney in August 2010, I was initially disappointed that I wasn't going to be put on the birth certificates. Yet we had a whole new mess on our hands after learning that neither of our names could go on them. It didn't make any sense. If Nathan denied paternity—which he would—then who was the father of these babies? Either the hospital records woman was lying or our attorney was.

We frantically called Janice, our attorney. We hadn't communicated with her since our first meeting, because there was no reason to. She told us the legal paperwork had to be done after the birth of the children. Needless to say, we had lots of questions for her.

"Our babies were born yesterday," Cedric explained. "The hospital is refusing to accept any paternity documents because state vital records and hospital attorneys said not to. They are claiming they don't have to in our case. What are we supposed to do?"

The best advice our highly paid attorney, who had claimed to have knowledge about the legalities of surrogacy, could give Cedric was, "I'm not sure if anything can be done. If you find someone who knows, tell them to call me and explain it."

As calm as could be, he responded, "We will not be needing your counsel any longer. What do we need to do to make that official?"

"Well . . . uh . . . an e-mail would suffice," she stuttered.

"You'll be getting that very soon," he said.

We went from having a small problem of my name not being on the birth certificates to the huge dilemma of neither of us being listed on them. With Cedric not named as the father, the twins couldn't be covered under his insurance. We had just fired our useless attorney, who apparently had lied to us. We had no one else to help us and didn't even have a clue where to start. My response to the situation was less than ladylike. Our fairytale ending was not turning out the way I thought it would.

"What the crap do we do now?" I asked.

Cedric said, "You type an e-mail firing that idiot lawyer. Then start searching for another, preferably one who isn't so inept. I'll make calls to vital records and hospital administration to try to figure out what's going on."

I started typing a scathing e-mail. I gave her competence and character a thrashing from behind the safety of the keyboard and the computer screen. However, I didn't want to be sued for defamation, so I reluctantly erased my offensive rant and typed a generic, one-sentence version: WE NO LONGER NEED YOUR SERVICES.

My next task was to find an attorney who *could* help us. We needed one in a bad way. I had done hundreds of searches before the pregnancy, and the only attorney I could find was Janice. We needed another divine intervention quickly. I did an exhaustive Internet search for attorneys. I typed various words and phrases, hoping some of them would lead me to a legal rescuer. *God, we need your help. Give us someone.*

I stumbled across a law firm advertising that it served clients with matters of paternity. It wasn't surrogacy, but it was a starting point, considering we were currently fighting a paternity battle. Due to its being so late in the day, neither Cedric nor I had any luck contacting anyone we desperately needed to speak with. We would have to continue our search the next day.

Waiting was the story of my life. At least it gave me something to think about while I stayed up all night in a stupor, feeding one baby and then the other, over and over and over again. I realized I was getting old, because I was not capable of all-nighters as I had been ten years earlier. It was only the second night, and I wanted to cry from lack of sleep. Maybe my despair was actually from the nightmare we were living, not being able to claim our flesh and blood as our own. Either way, I was dejected.

A new day dawned, which was also the beginning of February. I hoped that maybe Cupid would shoot some people in their butts with his arrows and send some love our way. I called the prospective attorney while Cedric fought with the people at vital records. Things seemed to be going badly on his end. I hoped we would have better luck with the lawyer.

"We're the intended parents in a gestational surrogacy. The babies were born a few days ago. Our former attorney told us we had to file paternity documents after their birth. The hospital and state vital records are telling us my husband can't go on the birth certificate, regardless of what documents he signs. We are in desperate need of help."

"First of all," the woman said, "your attorney should have told you to have this paperwork filed beforehand. Furthermore, your husband and the surrogate's husband can sign those paternity documents and they are legal, regardless if this was a surrogate pregnancy or not. As far as the hospital or any other entity is concerned, it is a question of who the father is, not what kind of pregnancy it is. You yourself can't get on the birth certificate unless a judge signs a court order declaring you the biological mother. Some judges will, and others will not. If the latter is the case, then you will have to go through the adoption process to gain legal guardianship of your children. It really comes down to how friendly the judge wants to be. There is a document that you, your husband, the surrogate, and her husband will need to sign, agreeing to who the real biological parents are. Finally, the judge will hopefully sign what is called an Order of Parentage. It legally establishes you and your spouse as the parents. If I am your counsel, I will prepare the documents for you. This all can be worked out, but there is a lot that should have been accomplished already that wasn't. It may take a while."

I was so relieved. There was a lot to do, but at least she gave us a place to begin. She had answered all of our questions in a matter of minutes.

"We want you as our attorney!" I said.

"Okay. I'll send you an engagement letter today. It will summarize what we discussed, what I will try to accomplish for you, and the fees, of course. We'll get this done, one way or another."

"You are our saving grace. Thank you so much."

I was feeling a great deal more confident than I had been. She confirmed what the previous attorney had said about me adopting, but Mrs. Gabriel, the new addition to our team, connected the dots for us so that we could at least understand the issues. She even provided an unexpected ray of hope: I might be able to be on the birth certificate as the mother of my own babies after all. God had delivered. Surely, anyone with the name Gabriel could bring good news.

Cedric's phone call to vital records didn't fare so well. "I talked to a lady named Sharon Newbirth. Seriously, she answered the phone and said, 'This is Sharon Newbirth.'"

"That's ironic," I said.

"She said the same thing as the woman here in records. I can't go on the birth certificates. I read the Oklahoma statutes word for word to her. The law says the paternity documents are what is required to get my name on the birth certificates. She said if I sent them, she would throw them in the trash when she received them. The only document that would force her to accept them is a court order. She was not friendly or helpful."

It seemed as if the world was against us. We were encountering so many obstacles. Our only ally was Mrs. Gabriel.

"Call our new attorney," I said. "Tell her what you told me. She is going to help us."

Cedric called and rehashed everything.

"She doesn't understand the entire situation," our lawyer responded. "She files records one way and knows no other way because of sheer stupidity or laziness. Just send the paternity documents to her anyway—as soon as possible—and I'll get the court order."

We had never been involved in any type of legal circus—no divorces, lawsuits, bankruptcies, or even traffic tickets. This was unfamiliar to us, beyond frustrating, and very scary. The woman from hospital records came in on her broomstick soon after our telephone wars. By the pursing of her lips and the scowl of her face, we knew she didn't come to share good news. No pleasantries were exchanged.

"You will not be allowed to leave the hospital with the children," she said.

"What!" we both exclaimed. I started sweating, and my heart raced.

"You are not the birth parents, so you can't take them."

Cedric said, "That's fine. We'll just get Kourtney to take them out and hand them to us in the parking lot."

She looked bewildered but still retained an evil glare.

"You would do that?" she asked.

"Yep."

"Well, she can't have them either," she rebutted.

"And why is that?" he asked.

"Because she is not the biological mother."

This lady was either on a power trip because she had a legal team to back up what she was saying, or she was just really stupid.

"So no one can take them?" Cedric asked.

"That is correct. No one is going home with them."

"There is no logic to what you are saying," he said.

She crossed her arms. She shot daggers at us with her eyes. "That is just how it is," she responded.

"We'll see about that!" Cedric said.

I was coming uncorked. Our babies were going to be wards of the state, and we didn't know why. I'd thought the pregnancy was full of drama. That was nothing. Every person we faced—with the exception of Mrs. Gabriel—was uncaring, unsympathetic, and unwilling to take time to investigate our unique situation. I looked at my babies and contemplated sneaking them out of the hospital and into hiding. We were already being treated like criminals. I feared we might have to do something drastic.

"We need to call the attorney," I said, loud enough to make sure the records woman heard me on her way out.

I called Mrs. Gabriel in a frenzy. "We are being told we can't take the babies home, and the surrogate can't sign for us to take them home. They said even the surrogate wasn't allowed to take them out of the hospital."

"That is a bunch of bull," she said. "That is like false imprisonment. There has been no crime committed. If they don't tell you they made a mistake by the end of the day, they will have to deal with me, and I will go crazy on them."

The way words fell upon deaf ears with everyone else, I figured she would need to intervene soon.

☙❧

While we fought with tyrannical hospital administration personnel and state offices, the twins fought small battles of their own. Each day they lost a few ounces from their original birth weight. Until that stopped, we didn't have a choice but to stay in the hospital, regardless of what our adversaries told us. The minor weight loss was normal, but it needed to cease. Otherwise, the babies faced the possibility of being put on feeding tubes. In addition to feeding issues, jaundice affected their tiny bodies. Jaundice was somewhat common, even in full-term babies. It concerned the nurses but didn't warrant major intervention. We simply placed the babies in the sunshine coming through the window during the day and watched them bask like little lizards. In the evening they lay under special phototherapy lights that also helped remove any excess bilirubin remaining in their blood.

The evenings helped minimize the stress we endured during the days. We sat peacefully with no phone calls or interruptions and gazed at our twins sunbathing under the lights. We thoroughly enjoyed those short-lived moments. We had a lot of challenges ahead of us, but God had chosen us to be their parents. We felt an immense amount of joy. That alone made us want to stay in the fight. Before we went to bed, one of the nurses came in. I assumed that she wanted to check on the babies, but she addressed us instead.

"I thought you guys might like to know that you will get to take your babies home. Kourtney can sign a paper, releasing them to you."

"That is outstanding news," Cedric said, closing his tired eyes and letting out a sigh of relief.

"I'm not sure what happened earlier, but you were given bad information. We're very sorry for the mix-up."

We didn't know whether our attorney had called and raised hell or the hospital really had bad information. The news certainly delivered instant relief to us. We had failed to accomplish everything else, but at least we could bring our children home and not fear the law taking us into custody for kidnapping. I can't say we slept well that night, thanks to busy babies, but we savored the small legal victory.

twenty seven

Going Home

Groundhog Day brought six more weeks of winter—doesn't it always?—and another day of the babies' weight loss. We struggled to get them to eat. Every nurse, grandparent, and friend tried to help us. Our stubborn son refused to eat much, and, as a result, he had the greatest weight loss percentage. Laney's weight stabilized for the first time. We stayed busy feeding the babies and hoping for weight gain so we could go home.

We had to let the legal stuff shake out on its own. Our attorney did the dirty work for us. We prayed that she wouldn't create a disaster, as the last one had. Cedric escaped for a few hours to meet Nathan and our pastor, who served as a witness to the signing of the paternity documents. Cedric described it as the most undignified task he had ever performed. In the pouring rain, he and our pastor met Nathan at a rundown convenience store. The beer signs, the broken-down gas pumps, and posters proclaiming the current lottery status made the perfect venue for a preacher and two men to declare who the daddy was.

All three large men piled into the front seat of a pickup and passed around Denial of Paternity and Acceptance of Paternity forms. No one had ever questioned the paternity, but it humiliated Cedric to have to sign those types of documents. Let's face it, people who have to sign them usually have done something with someone they shouldn't have. Regardless, Cedric accomplished our legal part. We depended on our attorney to do the rest, through either a court order declaring parentage or the adoption of our biological children.

We spent several more days in the hospital because Brody kept losing weight. The walls started to close in. The pediatrician threatened to insert a feeding tube if he didn't stabilize and start gaining within twenty-four hours. We tried every technique and every person. Nothing worked. It frustrated us and scared us at the same time.

We sent out messages through texts and social media for people to pray for Brody. I found myself too exhausted to pray. I fell short in my prayers and literally fell asleep many times before getting any words out. I hadn't much to give God, but I knew he always waited and listened for me. He knew what was in my heart.

When the nurses retrieved the babies for their baths and weight checks, Cedric and I said a quick prayer together. An hour later, they brought the babies back, along with two cards showing their measurements. Brody had finally gained.

"Looks like you guys will be busting out of here soon," one nurse said.

The stress that had plagued me for so long melted away. I had never looked forward to sleeping in my own bed, showering in my own bathroom, or cuddling with my babies in my own chair more than I did at that moment. We finally had babies to take home. We had the family we had yearned for and sacrificed for. With God's precious miracles in hand, my soul filled up and overflowed with joy. Home would make parenting the children so much more real and special.

❧❧

The hospital officially discharged the babies a few days later, on February 6. When I first went outside, the brisk winter air hit my skin and chilled me to the bone. Yet once we walked out of the hospital's shadows and into the brightly shining sun, the magnificent bundles we carried into our new life were evidence of our glorious exit from the dramatic journey.

For years, the groundhog's prediction of six more weeks of winter had depressed me. However, the lifeless frigid season of long nights and air that was so cold it hurt to breathe provided God with the opportunity to show me how he can majestically transform the seemingly dead into life. He had a time for everything. From the beginning, our lives were carefully planned. We each had a route that he crafted especially for us. We did not know where it went, what obstacles might impede us, or how far we had to go to reach the end. Only one thing was for sure: that God always provided the tools we would need to weather any storms along the way. His grace abounds.

My years of struggle—my darkest seasons—had been created not on a whim or by chance. No. God had planted specific people at specific times in specific places to lay the stepping-stones in my path that led to the revealing of his miracles. Had I never taken a job working with Diane, had she never befriended me during my trials, Kourtney would not have come into my life. My babies would not exist. I would not have known about Jace. I would not have lent an empathetic ear to Kourtney. Kate's appendicitis may have gone undiagnosed and led to her death. Many call those random coincidences, saying that they only happened due to chance. Well, God did an outstanding job of morphing those *random coincidences* into two miraculous winter butterflies whom I get to call my own. God gave me quite a story to tell.

Epilogue

On March 19, 2012, Cedric and I became the legal birth parents of Brody and Laney via court order. We did not have to go through a lengthy adoption process, and both of our names went on the birth certificates. I got the honor of meeting Sharon "Newbirth" in person when I picked up the official birth certificates. Her last name wasn't Newbirth, by the way. New Birth was her department name. Cedric got a good jabbing for that one.

When I recorded these events in 2014, the twins were two years old and kept me very busy as a stay-at-home mom. I couldn't imagine being so blessed and not taking advantage of it. The once spotless house I grew up in has been seasoned with more love, more joy, and many stains, flaws, dents, and dings. Life is good.

Kourtney never tried to steal my babies, as I'd once feared. In fact, she went on to conceive another child soon after giving birth to the twins. She successfully delivered a healthy baby girl, Adley Jace, on January 14, 2013, slightly less than one year after the twins were born. We remain friends and still have occasional spats.

Our other two embryos are patiently waiting to find another surrogate, out of the state of Oklahoma this time.

Our sovereign God chose me, his imperfect messenger, to deliver this account and to encourage another soul who cries out to him, seeking answers and his will. It is to someone who is experiencing his or her darkest days, barely clinging on, and wondering whether he is there. God uses the broken, the flawed, and the weak—whether physically, mentally, or spiritually—so that he can demonstrate his unconditional love and his power to transform. Loving God is sometimes not easy. Understanding God is impossible, but he will provide a rainbow after the storm . . . in his time.

About the Author

Kenzie Janzen is a busy mom to Kate, Brody, and Laney and helps maintain the family farm in Oklahoma. She received her BS in Biological Sciences from Oklahoma State University and a MEd in Secondary Education from Northwestern Oklahoma State University. Before becoming a stay at home mom, Kenzie served as an officer in the U.S. Air Force. She also taught secondary science and math at several rural schools in Oklahoma. Her latest endeavor is writing a children's book about heaven. She can be contacted at ckkjanzen@gmail.com or www.kenziejanzen.com.